Are You Ready for Kindergarten?

Coloring
Skills

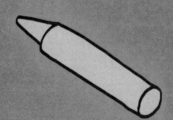

To parents: Coloring Skills

In this section your child will complete activities designed for mastering crayon control, which is a precursor to writing. This will nurture your child's understanding of colors and improve finger strength and dexterity – skills necessary for writing letters and numbers later on.

First, your child will scribble so that he or she can have fun with crayons and new colors. Then, your child will practice choosing the proper color crayon and coloring in a designated blank area. Your child will also practice drawing lines by connecting matching objects. Gradually, your child will color more neatly and firmly as his or her abilities improve. Coloring is a fun way for children to learn how to properly hold and use a writing utensil.

This skill will take plenty of practice to master. If your child struggles with any particular part of this section, please refer to the appropriate book from our other preschool products for more focused work.

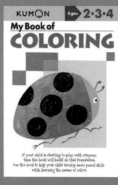 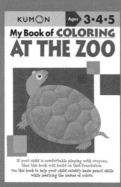  

My Book of COLORING   My Book of COLORING   Let's Color!   MORE Let's Color!
                             AT THE ZOO

How to hold a crayon properly

It is okay for your child to hold the crayon in his or her fist at first, but you should gradually teach your child to hold the crayon correctly.

Show your child how to hold the crayon close to the tip. This will prevent the crayon from breaking and will help your child practice the proper way to hold a pencil or other writing utensil.

In the beginning, do not worry too much about your child breaking the crayon or holding it properly. Observe your child's progress, and encourage him or her to advance one step at a time.

1 Big Tree

Name   Date

≺ example ≻

green ▶

■ Draw the leaves on the tree.

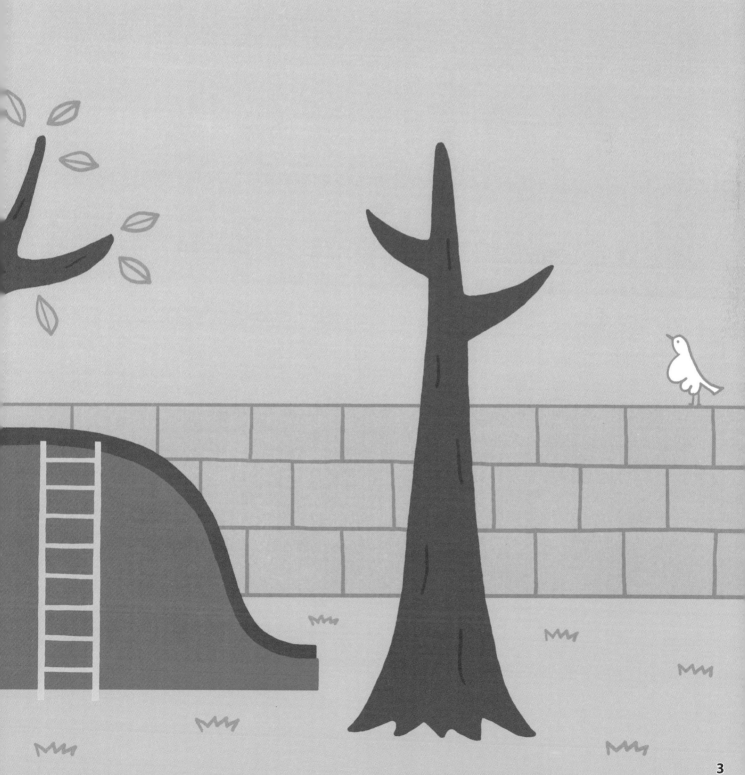

3

Blue Sky

< example >

■ Draw the clouds in the sky.

white

Walk in the Field

Name   Date

To parents   From this page on, your child will practice filling in a white area. The color of the sample crayon is just a reference. If you don't have the same crayon, it is okay to use a similar color or any color your child likes.

≪ example ≫

■ Color the white circle.

blue ▶

5

To parents In this exercise your child will practice drawing lines and improve his or her crayon control skills. It is okay for your child to choose a crayon that he or she likes.

■ Draw a line from the arrow (↓) to the star (★) by connecting each 🧢.

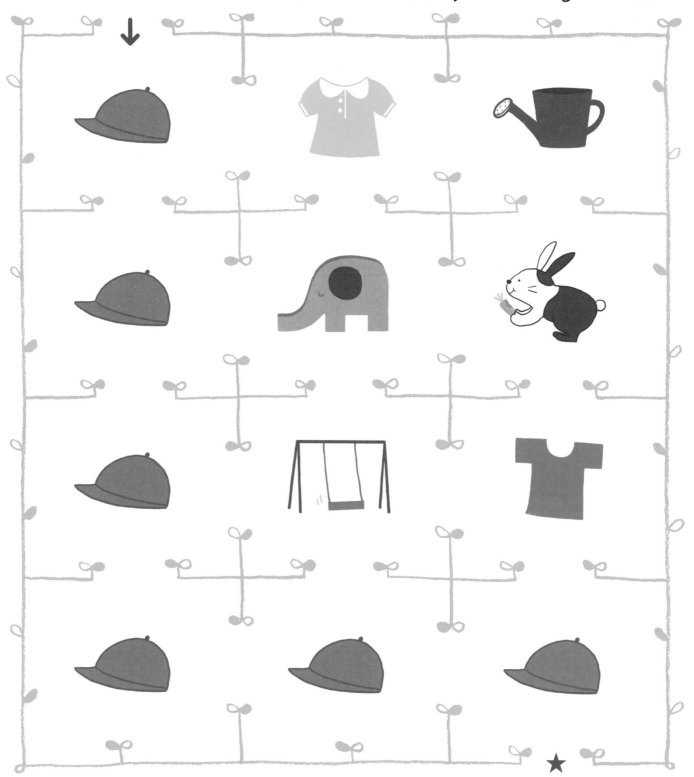

6

Hello!

Name..Date..

≪ example ≫

To parents It is okay if your child cannot color the entire white spot neatly. Do not be concerned if he or she colors outside of the lines. When your child is finished, tell your child to say "Hello" to the girl, too.

■ Color the white circle.

yellow ▶

■ Draw a line from the arrow (↓) to the star (★) by connecting each .

4 Slide

Name

Date

To parents The white square is designed to draw your child's attention to the shape of the slide. Encourage your child to color along the inside edges of the white square first, and then fill in the middle area.

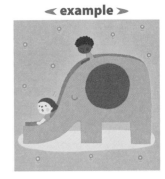

≪ example ≫

■ Color the white square.

violet ▶

■ Draw a line from the arrow (↓) to the star (★) by connecting each .

5 Swing

Name

Date

To parents First show your child how to color inside the edges of the white section, and then move to the middle. If he or she seems to be having difficulty, show your child what to do.

≪ example ≫

■ Color the white rectangle.

orange ▶

■ Draw a line from the arrow (↓) to the star (★) by connecting each .

Water the Plants

Name   Date

To parents   Your child will practice coloring a triangular area in this exercise. Encourage your child to color the inside edges of the white triangle first, and then complete the middle portion.

example

≪ example ≫

■ Color the white triangle.

red ▶

■ Draw a line from the arrow (↓) to the star (★) by connecting each .

7 Rabbits

To parents Don't be concerned about coloring over the edges. What is most important is that your child enjoys coloring.

■ Color the white triangle.

brown ▶

■ Draw a line from the arrow (↓) to the star (★) by connecting each 🐰.

8 Running

Name

Date

To parents From this page on, your child will practice coloring several areas in each exercise. On this page, there are two blank areas. Encourage your child to color both areas.

< example >

green ▶ orange ▶

■ Color the white circles.

■ Draw a line from the arrow (↓) to the star (★) by connecting each 👕.

Sandbox

Name   Date

≺ example ≻

■ Color the white circle and square.

blue ▶   violet ▶

■ Draw a line from the arrow (↓) to the star (★) by connecting each 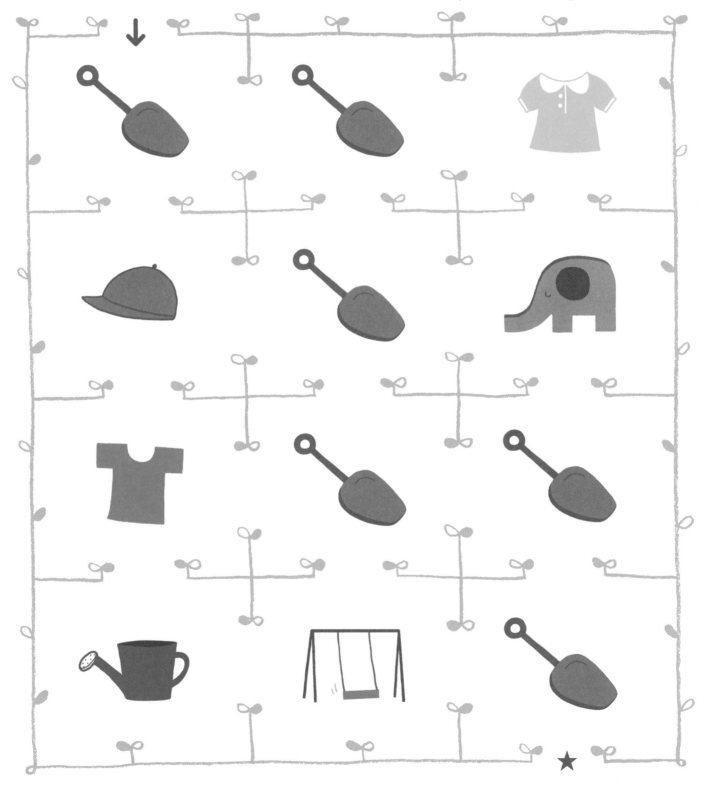.

< example >

■ Color the white circles and triangle.

blue ▶ orange ▶ red ▶

■ Draw a line from the arrow (↓) to the star (★) by connecting each .

11 Exercise

Name .... Date ....

To parents   It is important that your child becomes aware of shapes and colors. Talk with your child about the different shapes and colors in this illustration.

< example >

■ Color the white circle, triangle and square.

green ▸ orange ▸ yellow ▸

■ Draw a line from the arrow (↓) to the star (★) by connecting each 👕.

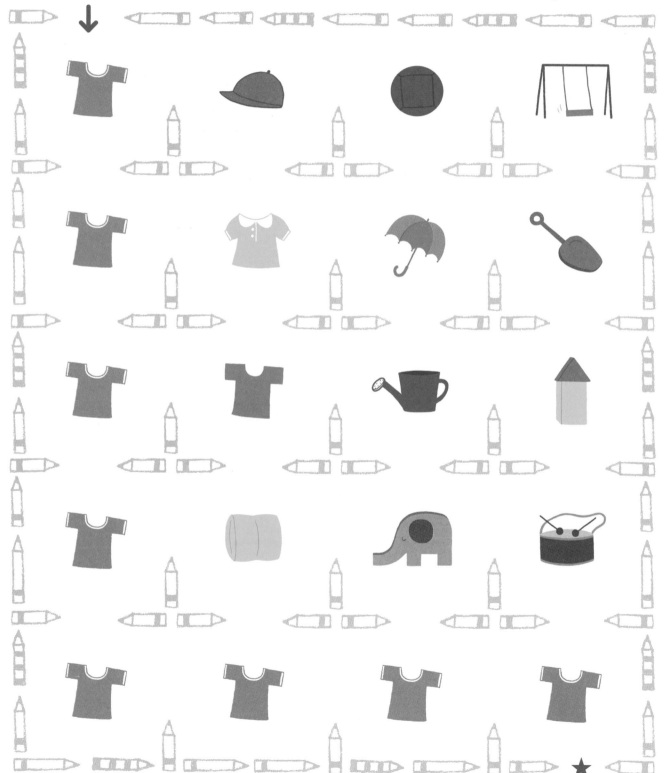

12 Big Blocks

Name   Date

To parents There are four white areas that your child will color on this page. Ask your child to choose which four colors he or she wants to use. It is okay if the colors your child chooses are different than the colors in the example.

≪ example ≫

■ Color the white circles and squares.

brown ▶ red ▶ violet ▶ yellow ▶

25

■ Draw a line from the arrow (↓) to the star (★) by connecting each 🏠.

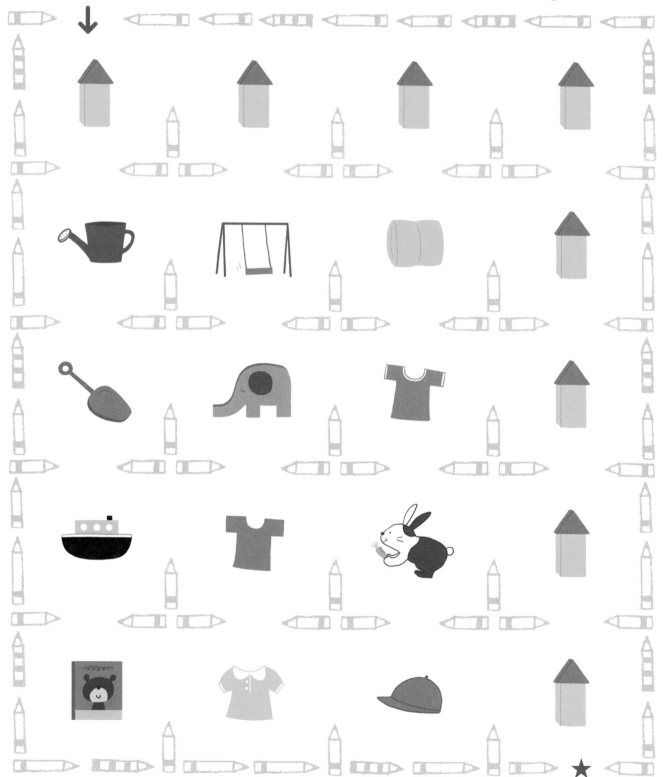

Rainy Day

Name .... Date ....

To parents   When your child is finished, praise his or her work and talk about the picture. You can say, "What colors are on the umbrella?" or "What color is the raincoat?"

≪ example ≫

■ Color the white circles, triangle and square.

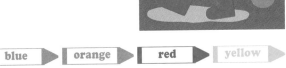

blue ▶ orange ▶ red ▶ yellow ▶

■ Draw a line from the arrow (↓) to the star (★) by connecting each ☂.

14 Pool

Name .... Date ....

To parents If you have been to a pool together, talk with your child about the fun time you had as he or she colors the picture.

≺ example ≻

■ Color the white circle, triangles and square.

blue ▶ orange ▶ red ▶ yellow

■ Draw a line from the arrow (↓) to the star (★) by connecting each ▨.

Lunchbox

Name .... Date ....

To parents There are five white areas that your child will color on this page. When your child has finished, talk about his or her favorite food in this lunchbox.

■ Color the white circles, triangle and squares.

brown ▶ green ▶ orange ▶ red ▶ yellow ▶

■ Draw a line from the arrow (↓) to the star (★) by connecting each 🍪.

Chicken

Name   Date

To parents   From this page on, each exercise will require more careful coloring. In this exercise, your child will color only one section.

< example >

■ Color the chicken's comb.

red ▶

■ Draw a line from the arrow (↓) to the star (★) by connecting each 🐔.

Concert

To parents Your child will color the drum in this picture. When your child is finished, you can talk about his or her favorite instrument.

< example >

■ Color the drum.

brown ▶

■ Draw a line from the arrow (↓) to the star (★) by connecting each 🥁.

 **Toy Box**

Name .... Date ....

To parents Your child will color the toy ship in this picture. When he or she is finished, say, "What a good boy! He is putting his toys away."

< example >

■ Color the ship.

black ▶

■ Draw a line from the arrow (↓) to the star (★) by connecting each ⛴.

Library

Name   Date

< example >

To parents From this page on, your child will color several more intricate areas. It is okay if he or she chooses colors that are different than the colors in the example.

■ Color the picture books.

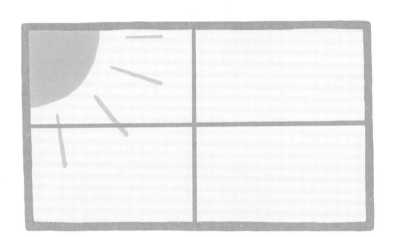

■ Draw a line from the arrow (↓) to the star (★) by connecting each .

To parents When your child has finished this page, offer lots of praise. You can say, "Good kids wash their hands often—just like you do, too."

< example >

■ Color the towel and soap.

green ▶   yellow ▶

To parents From this page on, the maze activities become more intricate. If your child is having difficulty, please guide your child by asking, "Where is the next yellow bar of soap?" When your child has completed the exercise, praise his or her hard work.

■ Draw a line from the arrow (↓) to the star (★) by connecting each .

Brush Your Teeth

Name   Date

‹ example ›

To parents Your child will color the cup and toothpaste. When your child completes this page, you can say, "What a good boy! He is brushing his teeth before bed. You brush your teeth then, too."

■ Color the cup and toothpaste.

blue ▶ yellow ▶

■ Draw a line from the arrow (↓) to the star (★) by connecting each .

22 School Bus

Name

Date

To parents The area your child will color is larger than the previous page. When he or she has finished, offer lots of praise, such as, "Wow! You colored a lot."

■ Color the bus.

black ▶ yellow ▶

■ Draw a line from the arrow (↓) to the star (★) by connecting each 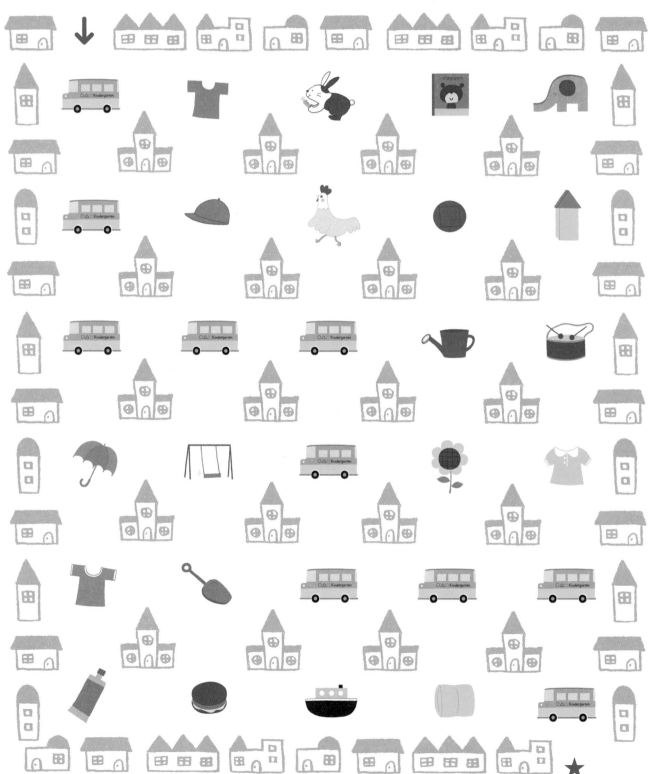.

23 Sunflowers

Name

Date

To parents Your child will color sunflowers. The white areas are intricate. If he or she colors outside the lines, it is okay.

< example >

■ Color the sunflowers.

brown ▶ yellow ▶

■ Draw a line from the arrow (↓) to the star (★) by connecting each 🌻.

24 Valentine's Day

Name .... Date

< example >

■ Color the hearts.

red ▶ violet ▶ yellow ▶

To parents From this page on, the maze activities include plain shapes instead of objects. If your child is having difficulty distinguishing shapes, try using *Kumon Shapes Write & Wipe Flashcards*. Also, please don't forget to praise your child's hard work.

■ Draw a line from the arrow (↓) to the star (★) by connecting each ●.

Birthday Cake

Name .... Date

To parents Your child will color a birthday cake in this picture. When he or she is coloring, you can say, "What kind of cake do you like?"

■ Color the cake.

red ▶ yellow ▶

■ Draw a line from the arrow (↓) to the star (★) by connecting each ●.

26 Paper Airplanes

Name Date

To parents From this page on, your child can choose any colors he or she likes. It is also okay to use a single color. Encourage your child to color independently until he or she is finished.

< example >

■ Color the paper airplanes with your favorite colors.

■ Draw a line from the arrow (↓) to the star (★) by connecting each ▲.

27 Flying Kites

Name

Date

To parents   On this page, your child will color the kites. Your child can choose a different color for each shape or kite, or use his or her favorite color for them all. Encourage your child to color independently.

≪ example ≫

■ Color the kites with your favorite colors.

■ Draw a line from the arrow (↓) to the star (★) by connecting each ▲.

28 Hiking

Name .... Date ....

‹ example ›

To parents Don't be concerned if your child is coloring outside of the lines. Let your child be creative with the colors he or she uses.

■ Color the hats and tree trunks with your favorite colors.

■ Draw a line from the arrow (↓) to the star (★) by connecting each ■.

29

Trick or Treat

Name

Date

< example >

To parents Your child will color the Halloween costume. When he or she has finished, offer lots of praise.

■ Color the Halloween costume with your favorite colors.

59

■ Draw a line from the arrow (↓) to the star (★) by connecting each ■.

Santa Claus

Name··Date

< example >

To parents This picture shows Santa Claus and a reindeer. When your child is finished, talk about the different winter holidays.

■ Color the picture with your favorite colors.

■ Draw a line from the arrow (↓) to the star (★) by connecting each ◆.

< example >

To parents This is the last page in this section. When your child is finished, compare this page with his or her previous work. You will see a lot of progress in your child's ability to control a crayon, choose colors and color evenly.

■ Color the picture with your favorite colors.

■ Draw a line from the arrow (↓) to the star (★) by connecting each ◆.

Are You Ready for Kindergarten?

Pencil Skills

To parents: Pencil Skills

In this section your child will complete activities designed to help him or her master pencil skills, which are a precursor to writing letters and numbers. Basic mazes allow your child to develop spatial reasoning and practice the pencil-control skills necessary for writing letters and numbers.

First, your child will trace lines through colorful mazes following clear directional indicators. Gradually, your child will complete more difficult mazes as his or her abilities improve. Mazes are a fun way for children to learn how to properly hold and use a pencil.

This skill will take plenty of practice to master. If your child struggles with any particular part of this section, please refer to the appropriate book from our other preschool products for more focused work.

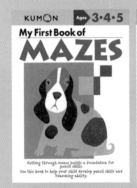  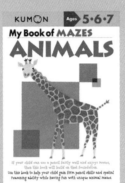  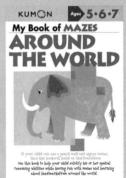

My First Book of MAZES   Amazing MAZES   My Book of MAZES: ANIMALS   My Book of MAZES: THINGS THAT GO!   My Book of MAZES: AROUND THE WORLD

How to hold a pencil properly

There are several ways to teach children to hold a pencil properly. Here is one example.

It can be difficult for a child who does not yet have enough strength in his or her hand and fingers to hold the pencil properly. Please teach this skill gradually, so that your child will remain interested and willing to hold a pencil naturally.

Help your child form an "L" shape with his or her thumb and forefinger as pictured here. Place the pencil against the top of the bent middle finger and on the thumb joint.

Now have your child squeeze the pencil with the thumb and forefinger.

Check the way that your child is holding the pencil against the example picture to decide whether or not it is the proper way.

Off to School

Name .... Date ....

To parents   This maze illustrates a walk around town. Children who are trying mazes for the first time can easily draw a line because the path is wide.

■ Draw a line from the arrow (➡) to the star (★) by following the path.

Going Home

■ Draw a line from the arrow(➡) to the star(★) by following the path.

2

A Trip to See Rabbit

Name   Date

To parents   It may help your child if he or she traces the path with his or her finger before using a pencil. However, the most important thing is that your child enjoys using a pencil with the maze.

■ Draw a line from the arrow (➡) to the star (★) by following the path.

Visit the Library

■ Draw a line from the arrow (➡) to the star (★)
by following the path.

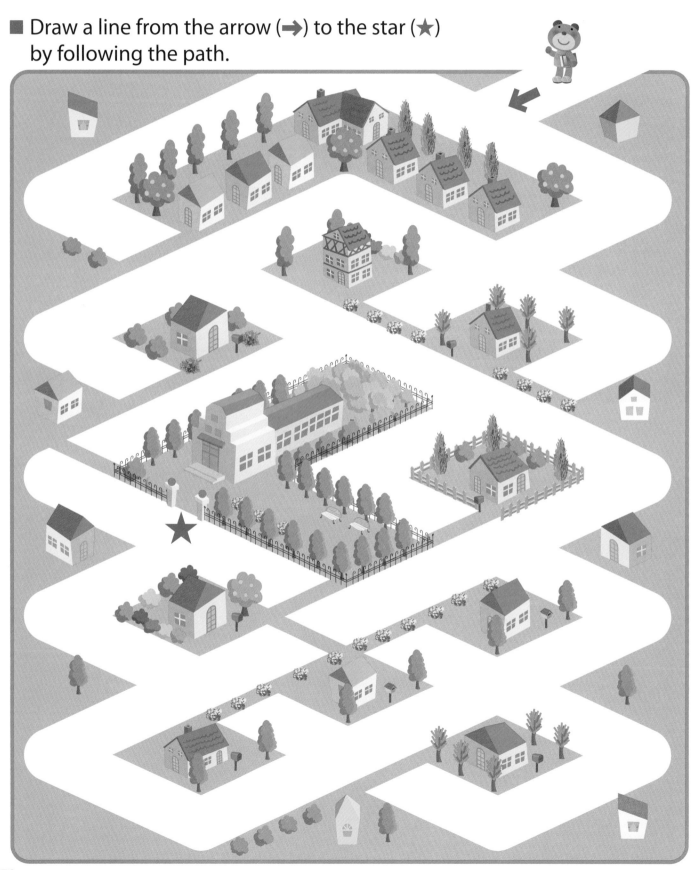

3 A Play Date with Giraffe

Date

To parents   It is okay if your child draws a line off the path. Offer lots of praise when your child arrives at the end of the maze.

■ Draw a line from the arrow (➡) to the star (★) by following the path.

Finding Cat's House

Draw a line from the arrow (→) to the star (★) by following the path.

Sending Mail at the Post Office

Name   Date

To parents Encourage your child to hold a pencil correctly. If he or she can not do so, hold the pencil with your child.

■ Draw a line from the arrow (➡) to the star (★)
by following the path.

73

On Our Way to the Park

■ Draw a line from the arrow (➡) to the star (★) by following the path.

Skip to the Seafood Store

Name   Date

To parents   When your child is finished, you can talk about the buildings in the town.

■ Draw a line from the arrow (➡) to the star (★) by following the path.

Buying Flowers

■ Draw a line from the arrow (➡) to the star (★) by following the path.

Let's Go Out to Eat

Name   Date

To parents   Don't forget that the most important thing is that your child enjoys using a pencil with the maze.

■ Draw a line from the arrow (➡) to the star (★) by following the path.

Run to the Bakery

■ Draw a line from the arrow (➡) to the star (★)
by following the path.

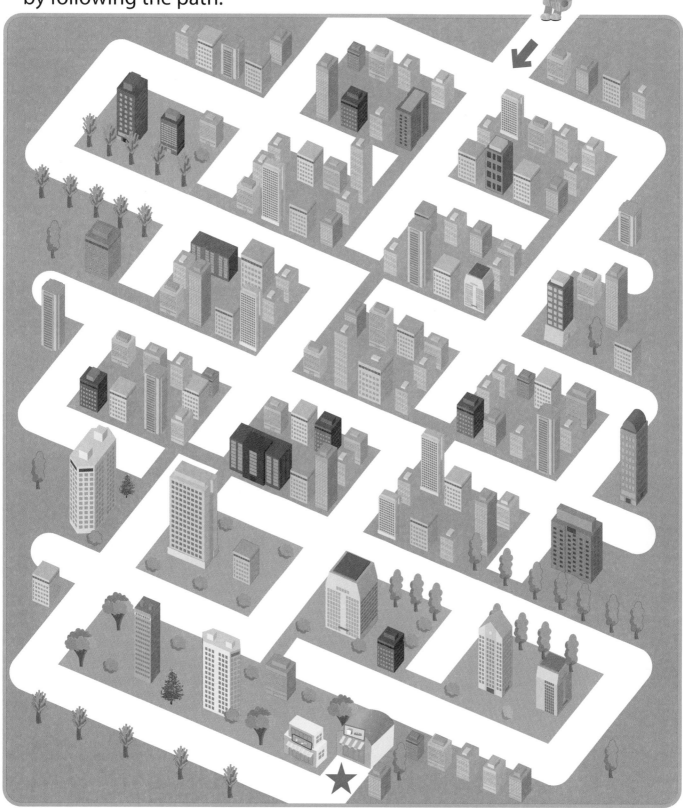

7 Soccer

Name .... Date ....

To parents From this page on, the mazes will become more difficult. Encourage your child to first trace the maze with his or her finger before using a pencil.

■ Draw a line from the arrow (→) to the star (★) by following the path.

Gymnastics

■ Draw a line from the arrow (→) to the star (★) by following the path.

8 Hopping

Name   Date

To parents   It is okay if your child cannot complete the maze neatly. When your child is finished, give him or her a lot of praise.

■ Draw a line from the arrow (➡) to the star (★) by following the path.

Ping Pong

■ Draw a line from the arrow (→) to the star (★) by following the path.

Birdhouse

Name

Date

To parents If your child is having difficulty holding the pencil, please hold it with your child.

■ Draw a line from the arrow (➡) to the star (★) by following the path.

Ride On Toy

■ Draw a line from the arrow (➡) to the star (★) by following the path.

Rainy Day

Name   Date

To parents   Don't forget to offer encouragement like, "You can draw a line very well!" Your child will enjoy using a pencil and completing mazes even more if he or she is praised.

■ Draw a line from the arrow (➡) to the star (★) by following the path.

Hopscotch

■ Draw a line from the arrow (➡) to the star (★) by following the path.

Wake Up!

Name

Date

To parents   The path of the maze will gradually become longer. When your child is finished, you can say "You wake up on time, too."

■ Draw a line from the arrow (➡) to the star (★) by following the path.

Toast

Draw a line from the arrow (➡) to the star (★) by following the path.

12 On My Way

Name   Date

To parents When the maze is complex, it is likely your child will go off the path. When your child arrives at the end of the maze without resting, offer lots of praise.

■ Draw a line from the arrow (➡) to the star (★) by following the path.

Unicycle

■ Draw a line from the arrow (➡) to the star (★) by following the path.

13 Jumping Rope

Name   Date

To parents   When your child is finished, you can talk about jumping rope and other fun activities. You can ask, "Can you jump rope?"

■ Draw a line from the arrow (➡) to the star (★) by following the path.

Baseball

■ Draw a line from the arrow (➡) to the star (★) by following the path.

Ice Skating

Name   Date

■ Draw a line from the arrow (→) to the star (★) by following the path.

At the Finish Line!

■ Draw a line from the arrow (➡) to the star (★) by following the path.

Marching Band

Name   Date

To parents   This is a complex maze. When your child is finished, offer lots of praise.

■ Draw a line from the arrow (➡) to the star (★) by following the path.

Pilots in Training

■ Draw a line from the arrow (➡) to the star (★) by following the path.

16 Halloween

Name

Date

To parents If your child seems to be having difficulty, you can help by asking, "Where is the next opening in the maze?"

■ Draw a line from the arrow (➡) to the star (★) by following the path.

Skateboard

■ Draw a line from the arrow (➡) to the star (★) by following the path.

17 Thanksgiving

Name

Date

To parents   Don't be concerned if your child cannot complete the maze in one try. What is most important is that your child enjoys the activity. You can ask your child, "What is your favorite Thanksgiving dish?"

■ Draw a line from the arrow (➡) to the star (★) by following the path.

Ice Hockey

■ Draw a line from the arrow (➡) to the star (★) by following the path.

100

18 Camping

Name .... Date ....

To parents The mazes are becoming much longer. Encourage your child to complete the maze. When he or she is done, give your child a lot of praise, such as, "Good job on finishing such a long maze!"

■ Draw a line from the arrow (➡) to the star (★) by following the path.

Cycling

■ Draw a line from the arrow (➡) to the star (★) by following the path.

19 Mother's Day

Name .... Date ....

To parents After completing the maze, talk with your child about different holidays and celebrations.

■ Draw a line from the arrow (➡) to the star (★) by following the path.

Hiking

■ Draw a line from the arrow (➡) to the star (★) by following the path.

Show Choir

Name   Date

To parents   How is the line that your child drew? Perhaps it is better than his or her previous work. Please tell your child how he or she is improving and offer lots of praise.

■ Draw a line from the arrow (➡) to the star (★) by following the path.

Football

Draw a line from the arrow (→) to the star (★) by following the path.

To parents   The mazes will gradually become longer. When your child arrives at the goal without resting, offer lots of praise.

■ Draw a line from the arrow (➡) to the star (★) by following the path.

Spin on the Teacup Ride

■ Draw a line from the arrow (➡) to the star (★) by following the path.

22 Playing Dress-up

Name

Date

To parents   This maze has many turns. Your child will need to use a pencil carefully, so watch him or her closely.

■ Draw a line from the arrow (➡) to the star (★) by following the path.

Basketball

■ Draw a line from the arrow (→) to the star (★) by following the path.

Santa Claus

Name   Date

To parents   It is good to talk with your child about each illustration. You can ask something like, "What is your favorite holiday?"

■ Draw a line from the arrow (➡) to the star (★) by following the path.

Gifts

■ Draw a line from the arrow (➡) to the star (★) by following the path.

24 Bus Trip

Name

Date

To parents   This maze is more complex than the previous maze. When your child completes this exercise, you can say, "You are great at mazes!"

■ Draw a line from the arrow (➡) to the star (★) by following the path.

Submarine

■ Draw a line from the arrow (➡) to the star (★) by following the path.

To parents   When your child is finished, you can talk about fire emergencies. You can start by saying, "When do people call a fire engine?"

■ Draw a line from the arrow (➡) to the star (★) by following the path.

Choo Choo!

■ Draw a line from the arrow (➡) to the star (★) by following the path.

To parents From this page on, the mazes will be an abstract pattern. These mazes have similar shapes, so they are more difficult than the previous mazes.

■ Draw a line from the arrow (➡) to the star (★) by following the path.

Twisting Maze

■ Draw a line from the arrow (➡) to the star (★) by following the path.

Zigzag Maze

Name

Date

■ Draw a line from the arrow (➡) to the star (★) by following the path.

Winding Maze

■ Draw a line from the arrow (➡) to the star (★) by following the path.

Spinning Maze

Name

Date

To parents This maze is made by combining curved lines. Your child may go at a slower pace because he or she must follow the circular shapes. Encourage your child to draw the path slowly and steadily.

■ Draw a line from the arrow (➡) to the star (★) by following the path.

Slanting Maze

■ Draw a line from the arrow (➡) to the star (★) by following the path.

Swivel Maze

Name

Date

To parents This maze is made by combining straight and curved lines. Encourage your child to draw the path slowly and steadily.

■ Draw a line from the arrow (➡) to the star (★) by following the path.

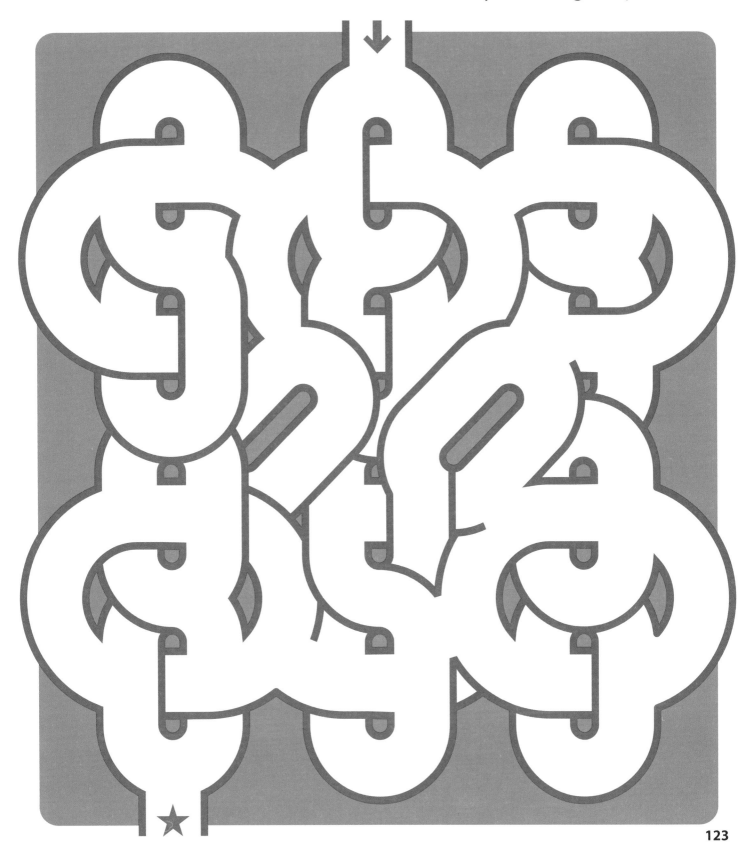

Turning Maze

■ Draw a line from the arrow (➡) to the star (★) by following the path.

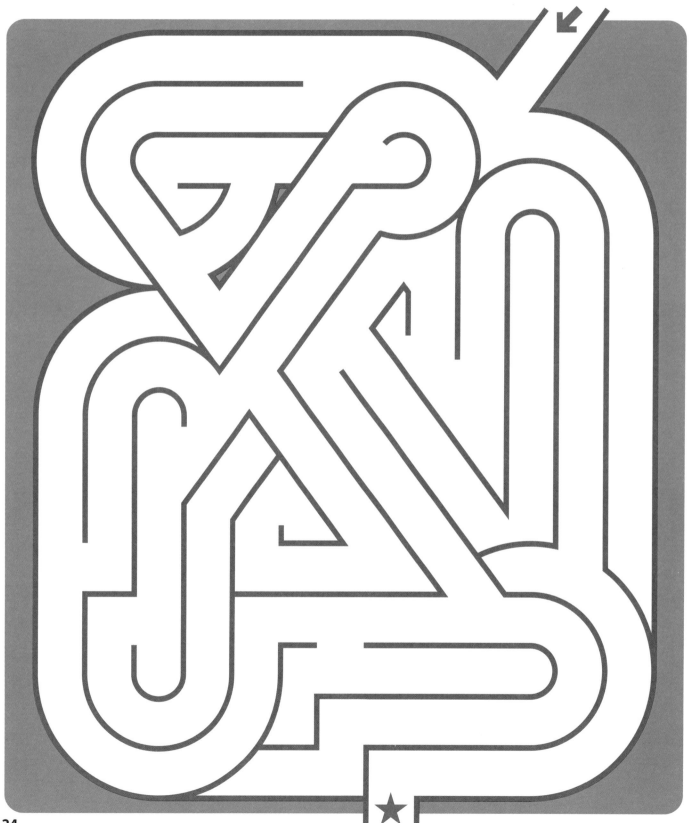

Whirling maze

Name   Date

To parents This maze is more complex. It is okay if your child cannot arrive at the goal without making a few mistakes. When your child is finished, offer lots of praise.

■ Draw a line from the arrow (➡) to the star (★) by following the path.

Twirling Maze

■ Draw a line from the arrow (➡) to the star (★) by following the path.

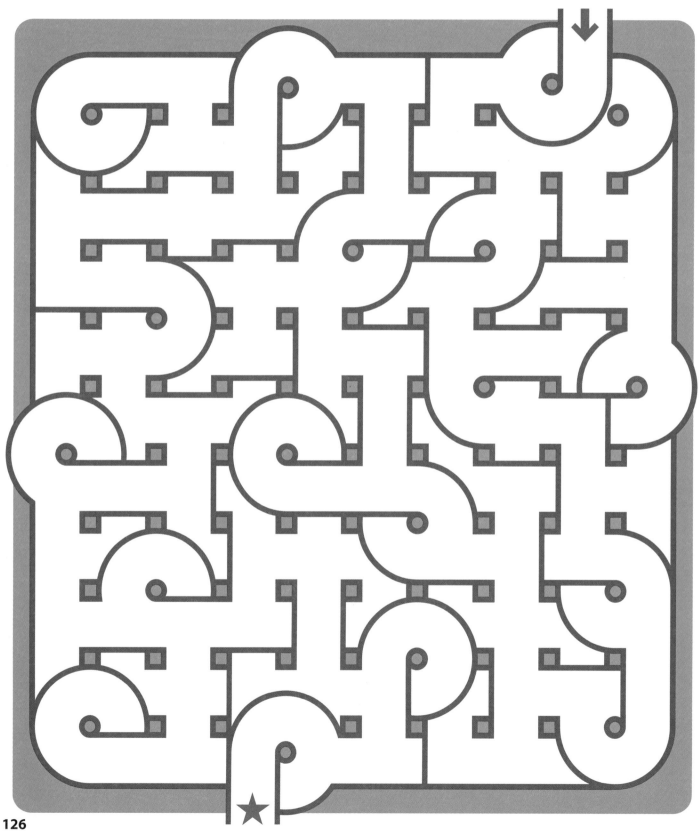

To parents This is the last page in this section. When your child has finished the book, compare this page with his or her previous work. You will see a lot of progress in your child's ability to use a pencil smoothly.

■ Draw a line from the arrow (➡) to the star (★) by following the path.

Mixed Maze

■ Draw a line from the arrow (➡) to the star (★) by following the path.

Are You Ready for Kindergarten?

Verbal Skills

A

Table of Contents

To parents: Verbal Skills

In this section your child will complete activities that will prepare him or her for the early reading skills he or she will learn in kindergarten. By practicing each of the verbal skills taught in this section, your child will be ready for academic success.

First, your child will learn alphabetical order step-by-step with uppercase and lowercase letters. Then, he or she will practice writing uppercase and lowercase letters. Next, your child will learn some early rhyming word pairs. Each topic is presented in Kumon's step-by-step method to allow your child to learn verbal skills without frustration.

This skill will take plenty of practice to master. If your child struggles with any particular part of this section, please refer to the appropriate book from our other preschool products for more focused work.

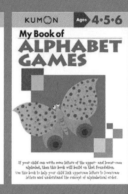

My First Book of
UPPERCASE LETTERS

My First Book of
LOWERCASE LETTERS

My Book of
ALPHABET GAMES

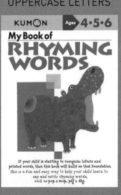

My Book of
RHYMING WORDS

Kumon Flash Cards
ABC's WRITE AND WIPE
Uppercase Letters

Kumon Flash Cards
ABC's WRITE AND WIPE
Lowercase Letters

How to hold a pencil properly

There are several ways to teach children to hold a pencil properly. Here is one example.

It can be difficult for a child who does not yet have enough strength in his or her hand and fingers to hold the pencil properly. Please teach this skill gradually, so that your child will remain interested and willing to hold a pencil naturally.

Help your child form an "L" shape with his or her thumb and forefinger as pictured here. Place the pencil against the top of the bent middle finger and on the thumb joint.

Now, have your child squeeze the pencil with the thumb and forefinger.

Check the way that your child is holding the pencil against the picture to help decide whether or not it is the proper way.

Uppercase Letters
Saying **A** → **E**

Name

....

Date

To parents If possible, have your child write his or her name in the box above. On this page, your child will connect the first five uppercase letters of the alphabet. From this page on, the number of letters will gradually increase. Please have your child say the letters aloud while he or she is tracing.

■ While saying each letter aloud, draw a line from Ⓐ to Ⓔ to connect the letters in alphabetical order.

| A | B | C | D | E |

■ While saying each letter aloud, draw a line from Ⓐ to Ⓔ to connect the letters in alphabetical order.

| A | B | C | D | E |

Uppercase Letters
Saying **A** → **J**

Name

Date

■ While saying each letter aloud, draw a line from Ⓐ to Ⓙ to connect the letters in alphabetical order.

| A | B | C | D | E | F | G | H | I | J |

■ While saying each letter aloud, draw a line from Ⓐ to Ⓙ to connect the letters in alphabetical order.

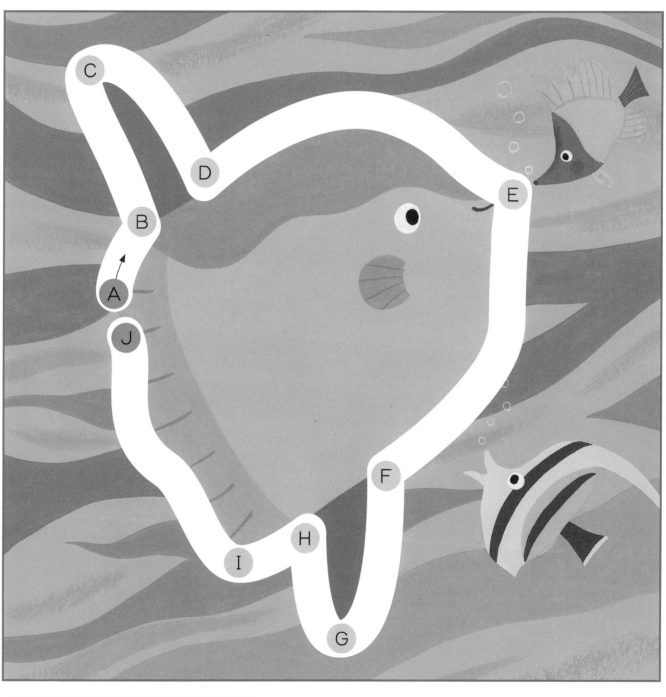

A	B	C	D	E	F	G	H	I	J

■ While saying each letter aloud, draw a line from (A) to (O) to connect the letters in alphabetical order.

| A | B | C | D | E | F | G | H | I | J | K | L | M | N | O |

■ While saying each letter aloud, draw a line from Ⓐ to Ⓞ to connect the letters in alphabetical order.

| A | B | C | D | E | F | G | H | I | J | K | L | M | N | O |

■ While saying each letter aloud, draw a line from Ⓐ to Ⓣ to connect the letters in alphabetical order.

| A | B | C | D | E | F | G | H | I | J | K | L | M | N | O | P | Q | R | S | T |

■ While saying each letter aloud, draw a line from Ⓐ to Ⓣ to connect the letters in alphabetical order.

A	B	C	D	E	F	G	H	I	J	K	L	M	N	O	P	Q	R	S	T

■ While saying each letter aloud, draw a line from Ⓐ to Ⓩ to connect the letters in alphabetical order.

| A | B | C | D | E | F | G | H | I | J | K | L | M | N | O | P | Q | R | S | T | U | V | W | X | Y | Z |

■ While saying each letter aloud, draw a line from Ⓐ to Ⓩ to connect
the letters in alphabetical order.

| A | B | C | D | E | F | G | H | I | J | K | L | M | N | O | P | Q | R | S | T | U | V | W | X | Y | Z |

6

Uppercase Letters
Writing **A** and **B**

Name
....
Date

To parents Before your child begins writing, please read the words on the page and ask your child to repeat them after you. If your child can recognize the letters, try having him or her tell you the name of each letter. In any case, please help your child say the name of the letter and its sound as he or she is tracing.

■ Trace the letters.

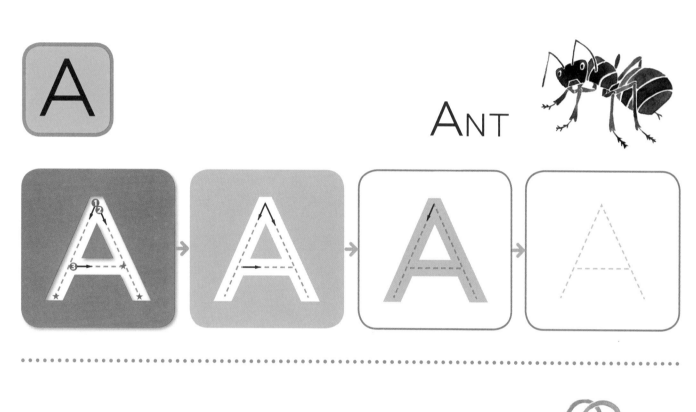

A   ANT

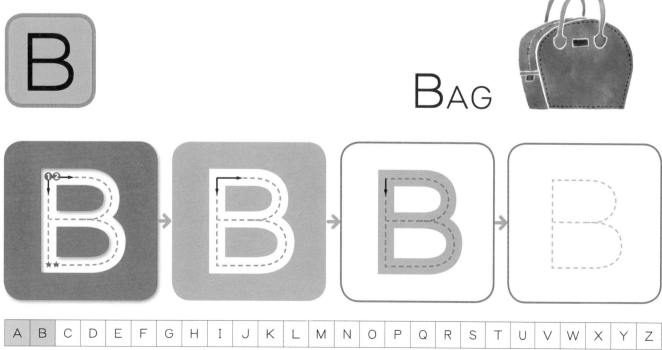

B   BAG

| A | B | C | D | E | F | G | H | I | J | K | L | M | N | O | P | Q | R | S | T | U | V | W | X | Y | Z |

Writing **C** and **D**

■ Trace the letters.

C   C<small>AT</small>

D   D<small>OG</small>

| A | B | C | D | E | F | G | H | I | J | K | L | M | N | O | P | Q | R | S | T | U | V | W | X | Y | Z |

■ Trace the letters.

E<small>GG</small>

F<small>OX</small>

A	B	C	D	E	F	G	H	I	J	K	L	M	N	O	P	Q	R	S	T	U	V	W	X	Y	Z

Writing **G** and **H**

■ Trace the letters.

GIFT

HAT

| A | B | C | D | E | F | G | H | I | J | K | L | M | N | O | P | Q | R | S | T | U | V | W | X | Y | Z |

Uppercase Letters
Writing **I** and **J**

Name

....

Date

To parents If your child is having difficulty tracing any of these letters, try our other workbooks, such as *My First Book of UPPERCASE LETTERS,* for additional practice.

■ Trace the letters.

INK

JAM

| A | B | C | D | E | F | G | H | I | J | K | L | M | N | O | P | Q | R | S | T | U | V | W | X | Y | Z |

Writing **K** and **L**

■ Trace the letters.

K_{EY}

L_{ION}

| A | B | C | D | E | F | G | H | I | J | K | L | M | N | O | P | Q | R | S | T | U | V | W | X | Y | Z |

146

Uppercase Letters
Writing **M** and **N**

Name

Date

■ Trace the letters.

M

Mat

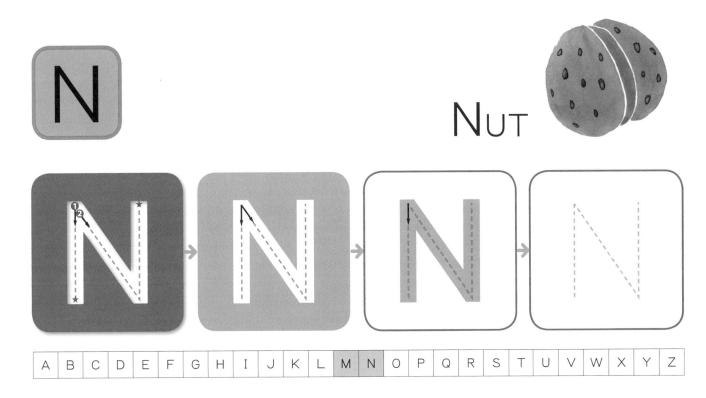

N

Nut

| A | B | C | D | E | F | G | H | I | J | K | L | M | N | O | P | Q | R | S | T | U | V | W | X | Y | Z |

Writing **O** and **P**

■ Trace the letters.

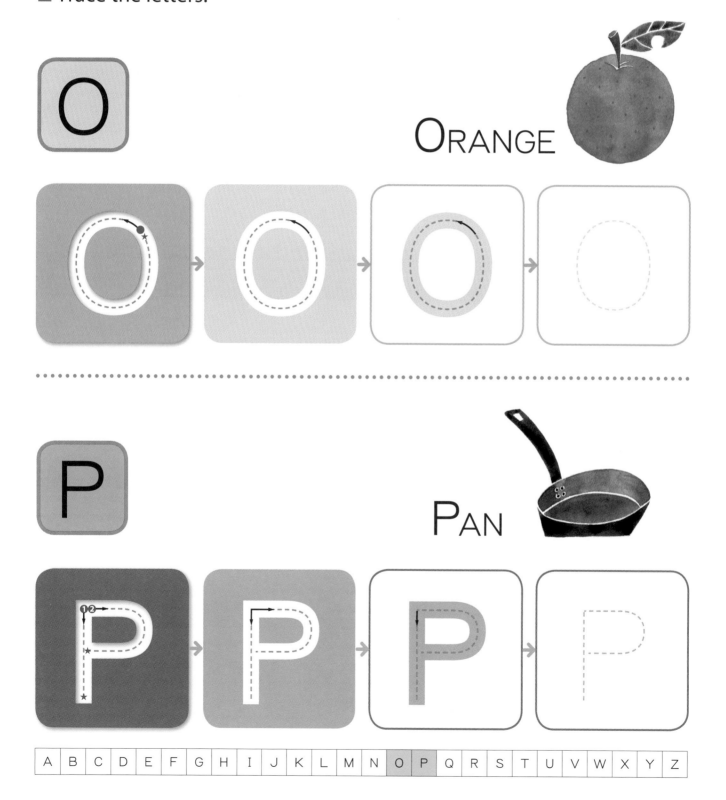

ORANGE

PAN

| A | B | C | D | E | F | G | H | I | J | K | L | M | N | O | P | Q | R | S | T | U | V | W | X | Y | Z |

To parents   Because of the way these letters are shaped, they are particularly difficult to write. Please praise your child for their hard work.

■ Trace the letters.

QUEEN

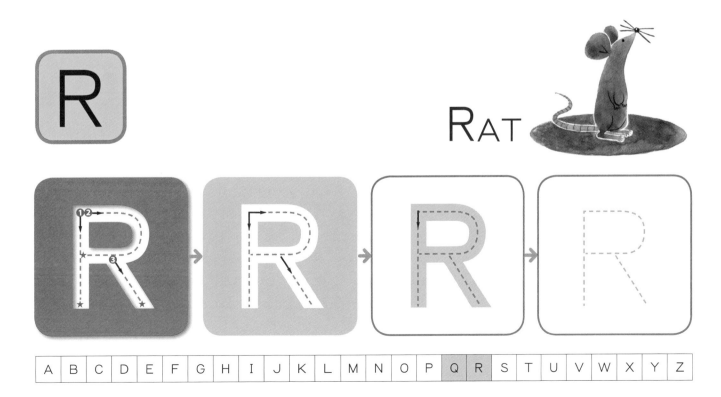

RAT

| A | B | C | D | E | F | G | H | I | J | K | L | M | N | O | P | Q | R | S | T | U | V | W | X | Y | Z |

Writing **S** and **T**

■ Trace the letters.

SUN

TOMATO

| A | B | C | D | E | F | G | H | I | J | K | L | M | N | O | P | Q | R | S | T | U | V | W | X | Y | Z |

■ Trace the letters.

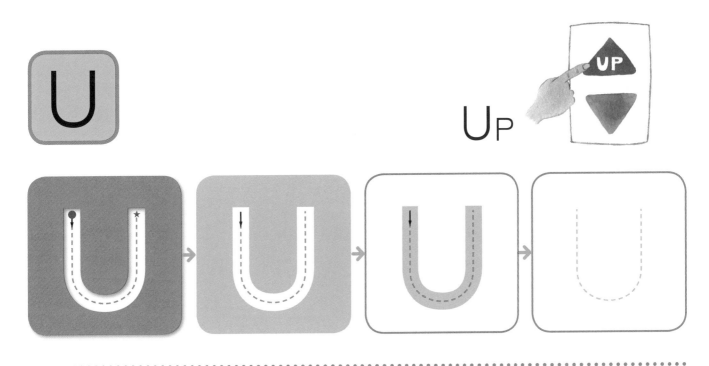

Up

Van

| A | B | C | D | E | F | G | H | I | J | K | L | M | N | O | P | Q | R | S | T | U | V | W | X | Y | Z |

Writing **W** and **X**

■ Trace the letters.

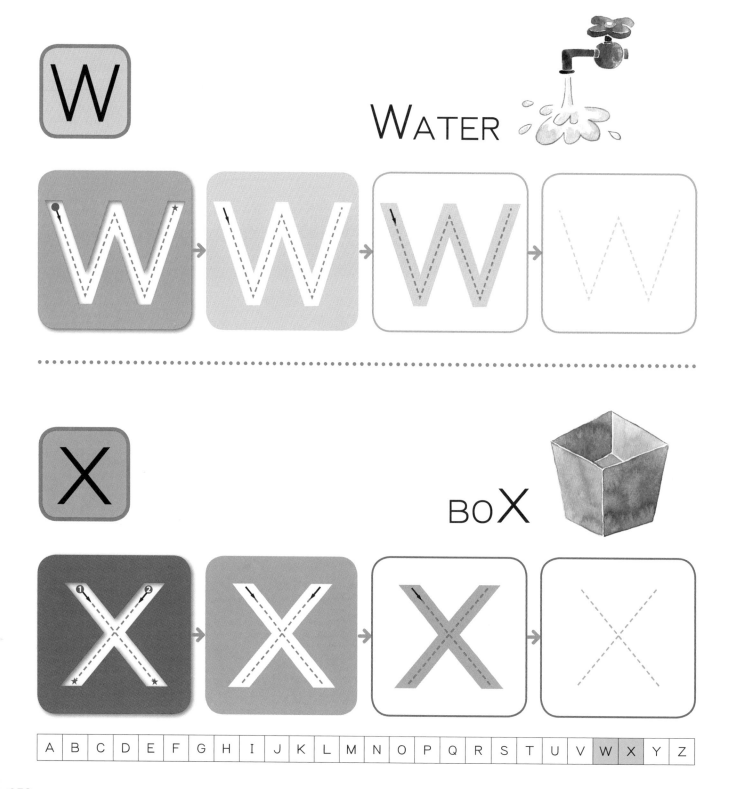

WATER

boX

12

Uppercase Letters
Writing **Y** and **Z**

Name
....
Date

■ Trace the letters.

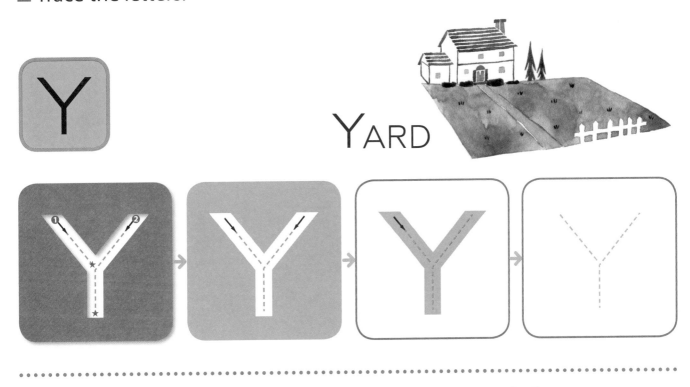

YARD

ZEBRA

| A | B | C | D | E | F | G | H | I | J | K | L | M | N | O | P | Q | R | S | T | U | V | W | X | Y | Z |

Review **A** to **Z**

■ Trace the letters in the table below.

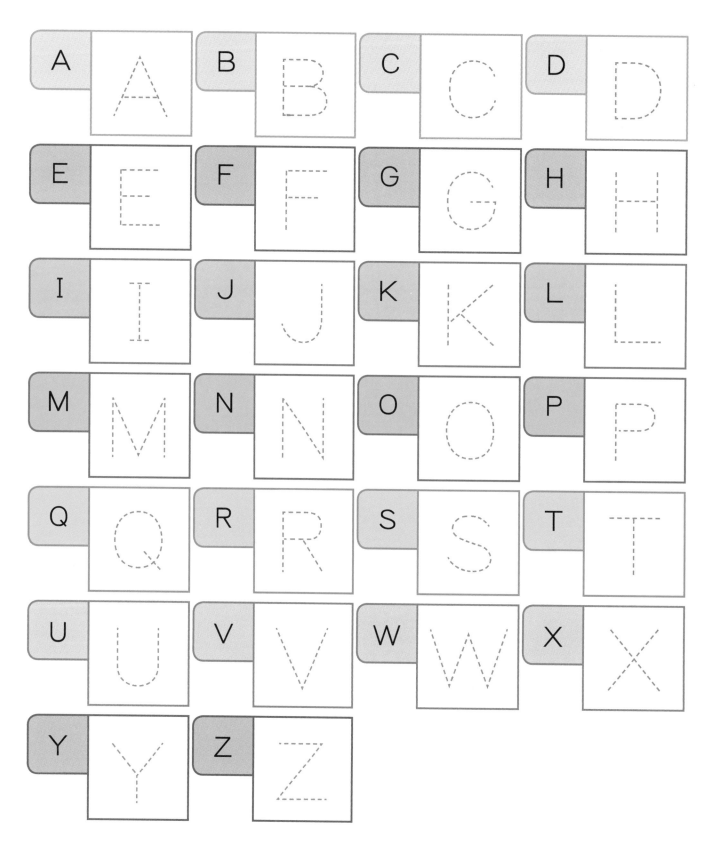

154

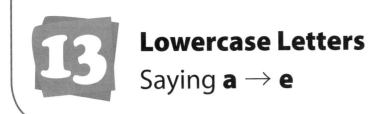

Lowercase Letters
Saying **a** → **e**

13

Name

Date

To parents   On this page, your child will connect the first five letters of the lowercase alphabet. From this page on, the number of letters will gradually increase. Please have your child say the letters aloud while he or she is connecting the dots.

■ While saying each letter aloud, draw a line from **a** to **e** to connect the letters in alphabetical order.

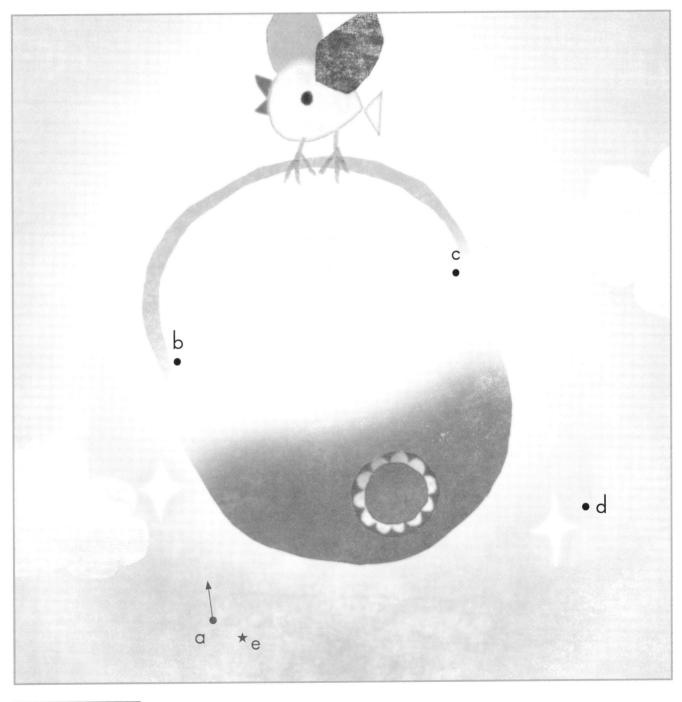

| a | b | c | d | e |

■ While saying each letter aloud, draw a line from a to e to connect
the letters in alphabetical order.

| a | b | c | d | e |

(boat)

■ While saying each letter aloud, draw a line from a to j to connect the letters in alphabetical order.

e

f

b

i

d

g

c

h

a

j ★

| a | b | c | d | e | f | g | h | i | j |

(dog) **157**

■ While saying each letter aloud, draw a line from a to j to connect the letters in alphabetical order.

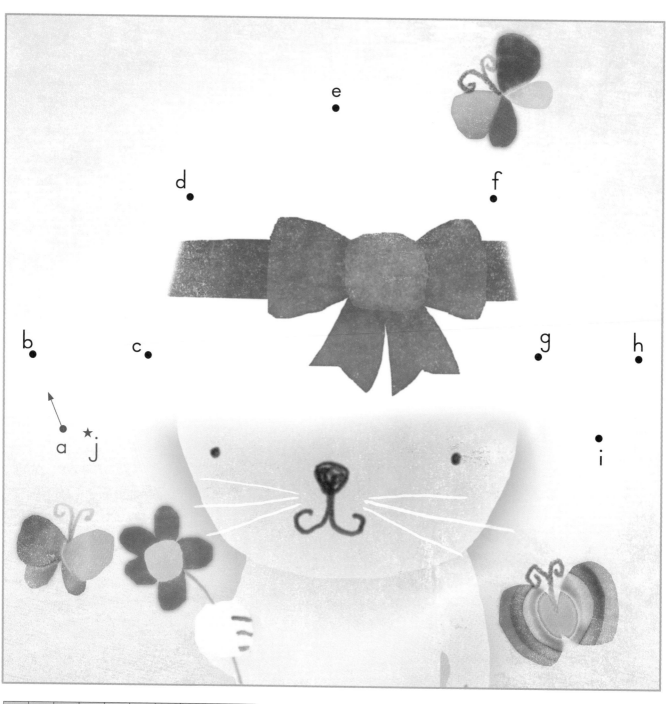

| a | b | c | d | e | f | g | h | i | j |

(hat)

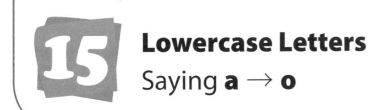
■ While saying each letter aloud, draw a line from a to o to connect the letters in alphabetical order.

| a | b | c | d | e | f | g | h | i | j | k | l | m | n | o |

■ While saying each letter aloud, draw a line from a to o to connect the letters in alphabetical order.

| a | b | c | d | e | f | g | h | i | j | k | l | m | n | o |

160   (whale)

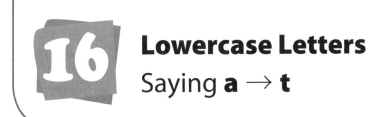

Lowercase Letters
Saying **a** → **t**

■ While saying each letter aloud, draw a line from a to t to connect the letters in alphabetical order.

| a | b | c | d | e | f | g | h | i | j | k | l | m | n | o | p | q | r | s | t |

■ While saying each letter aloud, draw a line from a to t to connect the letters in alphabetical order.

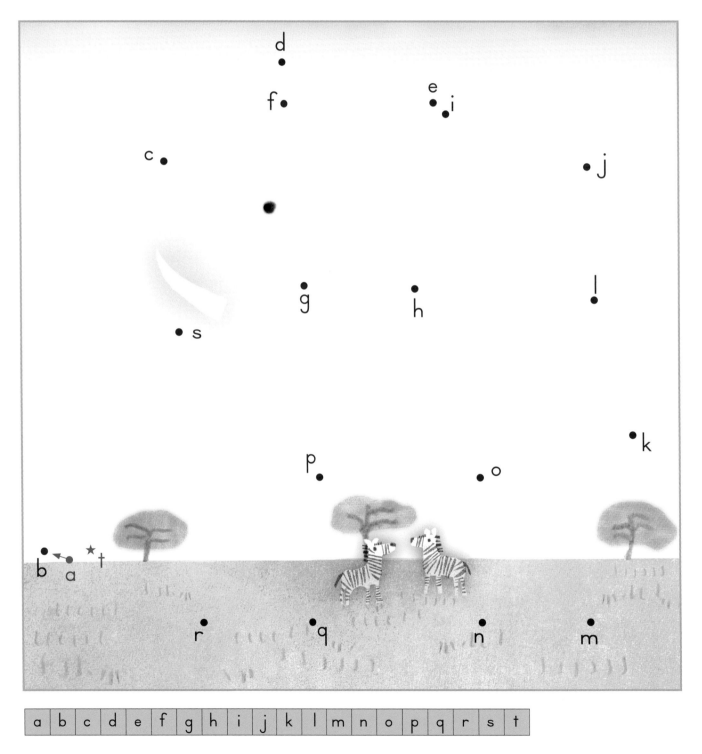

| a | b | c | d | e | f | g | h | i | j | k | l | m | n | o | p | q | r | s | t |

(elephant)

■ While saying each letter aloud, draw a line from a to z to connect the letters in alphabetical order.

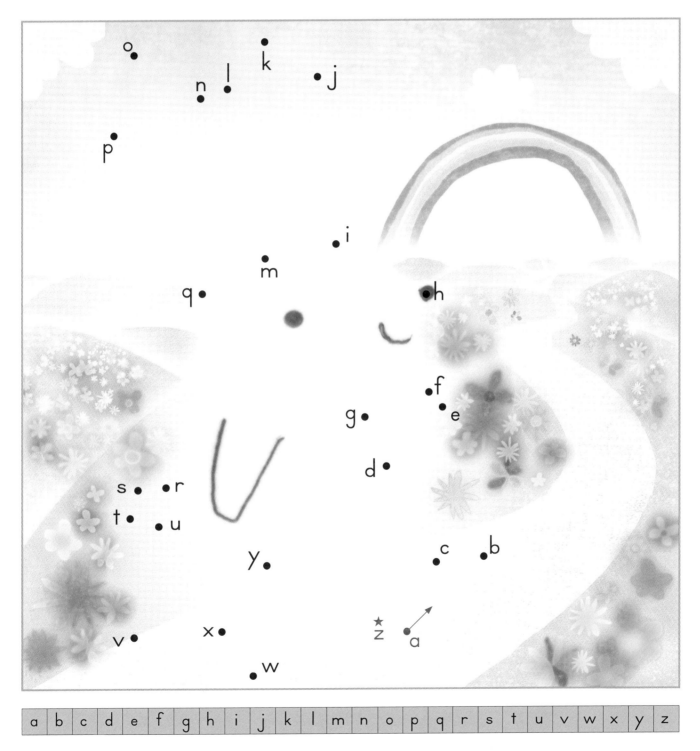

a	b	c	d	e	f	g	h	i	j	k	l	m	n	o	p	q	r	s	t	u	v	w	x	y	z

(rabbit) **163**

■ While saying each letter aloud, draw a line from a to z to connect
the letters in alphabetical order.

a	b	c	d	e	f	g	h	i	j	k	l	m	n	o	p	q	r	s	t	u	v	w	x	y	z

(rocket)

Lowercase Letters
Writing **a** and **b**

Name

Date

To parents Writing lowercase letters is even harder than writing uppercase letters. When your child completes an exercise, be sure to praise him or her.

■ Trace the letters.

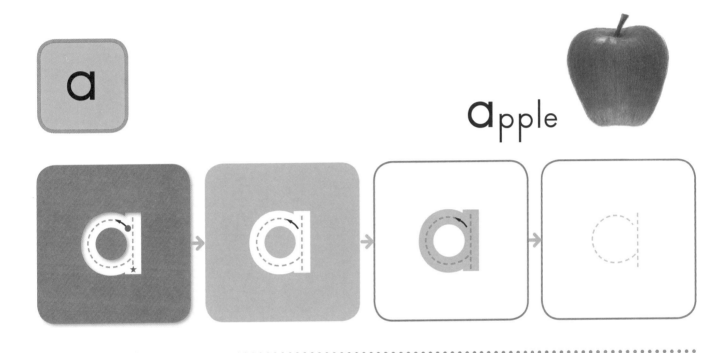

apple

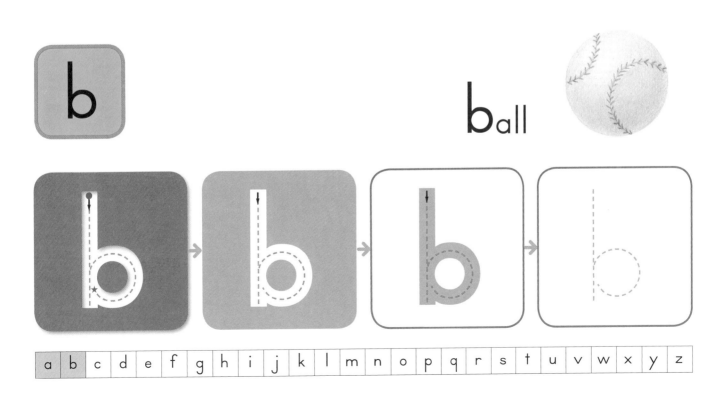

ball

| a | b | c | d | e | f | g | h | i | j | k | l | m | n | o | p | q | r | s | t | u | v | w | x | y | z |

Writing **c** and **d**

■ Trace the letters.

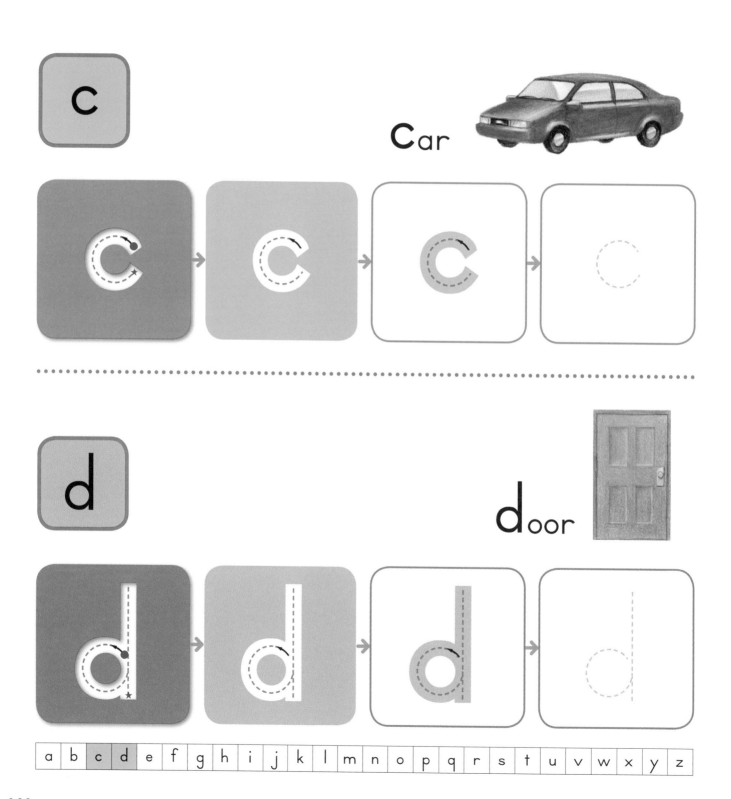

Car

door

| a | b | c | d | e | f | g | h | i | j | k | l | m | n | o | p | q | r | s | t | u | v | w | x | y | z |

■ Trace the letters.

e
ear

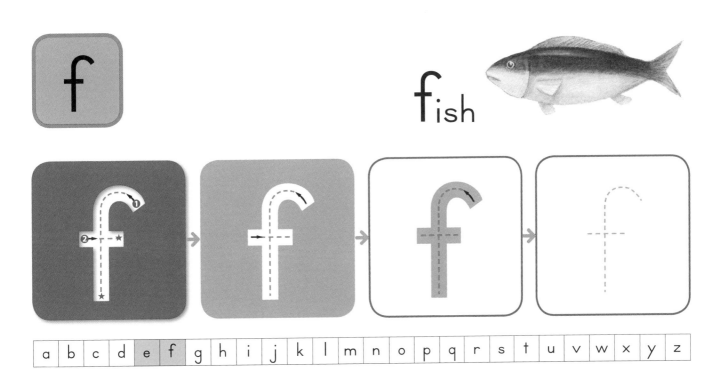

f
fish

| a | b | c | d | e | f | g | h | i | j | k | l | m | n | o | p | q | r | s | t | u | v | w | x | y | z |

Writing **g** and **h**

■ Trace the letters.

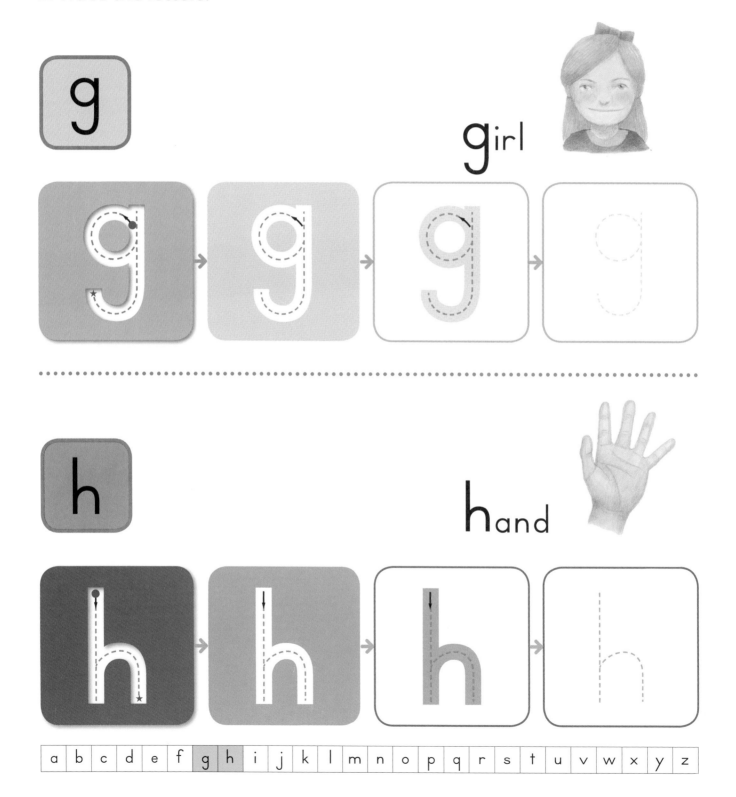

girl

hand

20

Lowercase Letters
Writing **i** and **j**

Name

Date

■ Trace the letters.

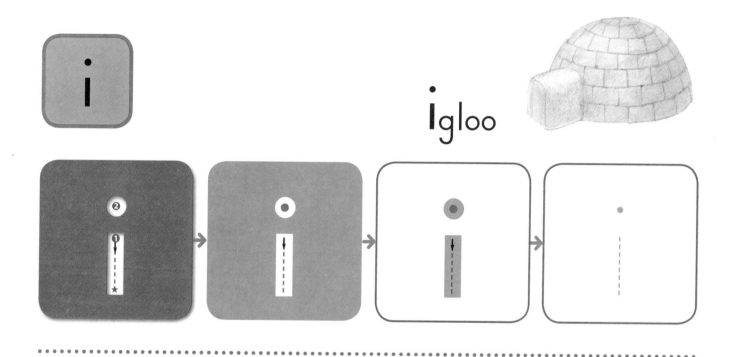

i

igloo

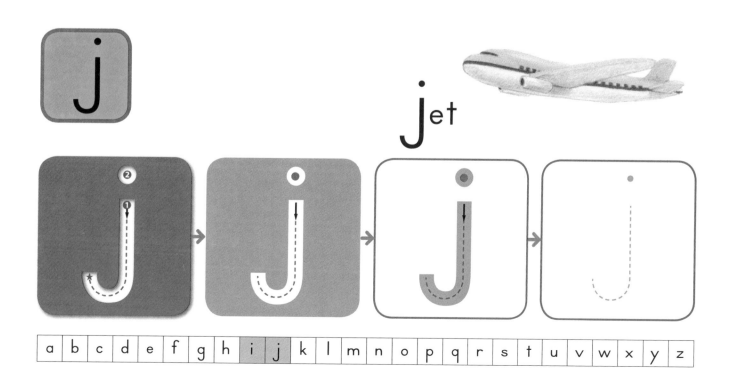

j

jet

| a | b | c | d | e | f | g | h | i | j | k | l | m | n | o | p | q | r | s | t | u | v | w | x | y | z |

Writing **k** and **l**

■ Trace the letters.

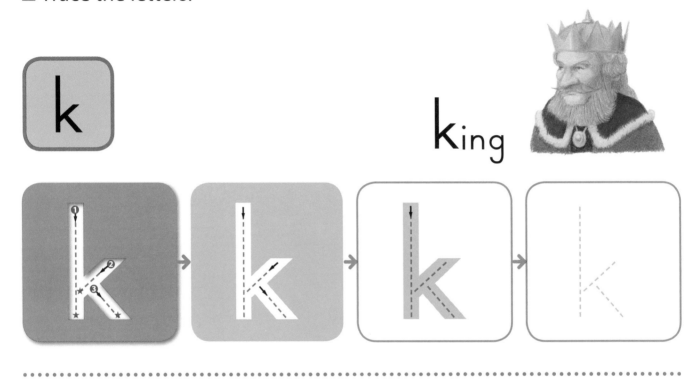

k_{ing}

l_{emon}

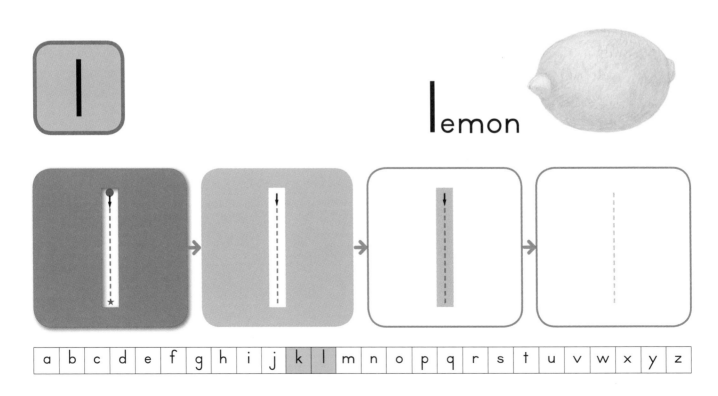

a	b	c	d	e	f	g	h	i	j	k	l	m	n	o	p	q	r	s	t	u	v	w	x	y	z

21

Lowercase Letters
Writing **m** and **n**

To parents If your child is having difficulty tracing any of these letters, try our other workbooks, such as *My First Book of LOWERCASE LETTERS,* for additional practice.

■ Trace the letters.

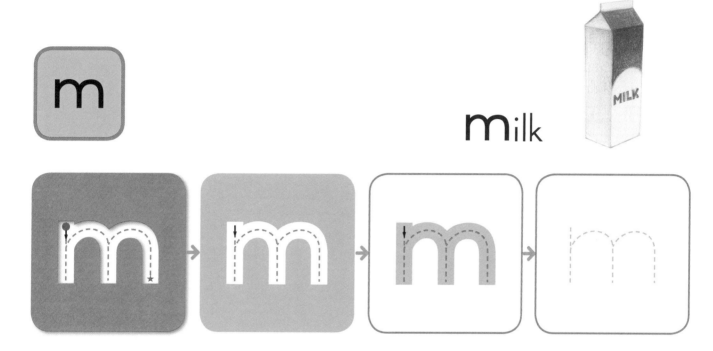

milk

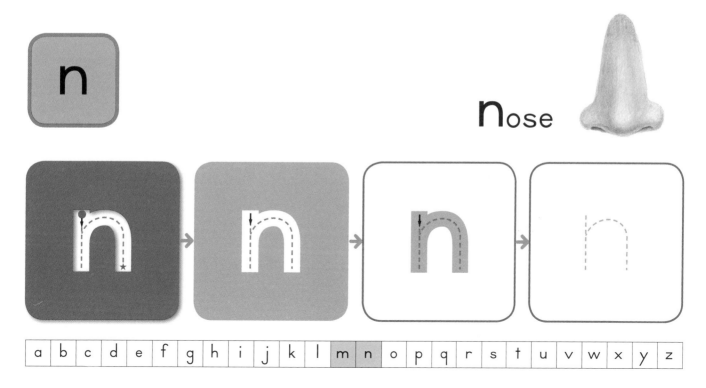

nose

a	b	c	d	e	f	g	h	i	j	k	l	m	n	o	p	q	r	s	t	u	v	w	x	y	z

Writing **o** and **p**

■ Trace the letters.

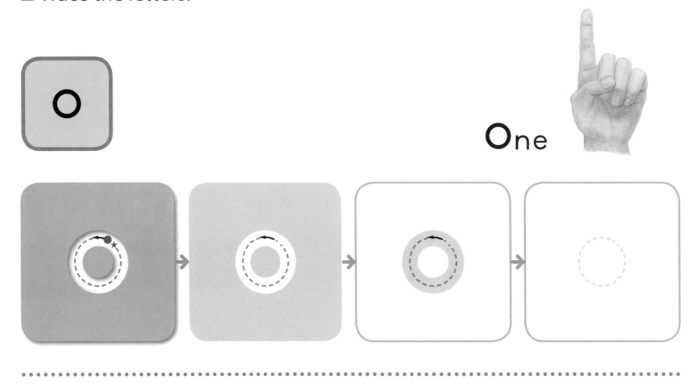

One

pig

| a | b | c | d | e | f | g | h | i | j | k | l | m | n | o | p | q | r | s | t | u | v | w | x | y | z |

22

Lowercase Letters
Writing **q** and **r**

Name

Date

To parents Because of the way these letters are shaped, they are particularly difficult to write. Please praise your child for their hard work.

■ Trace the letters.

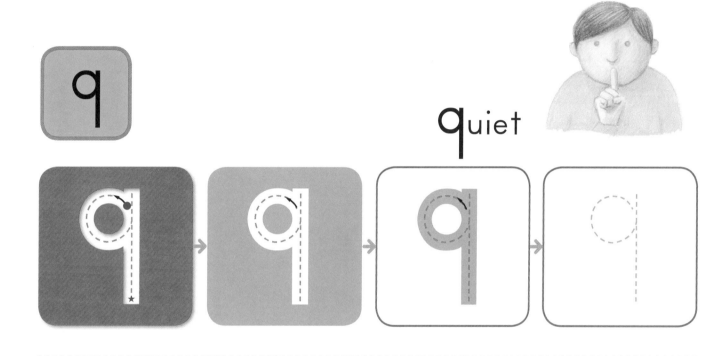

quiet

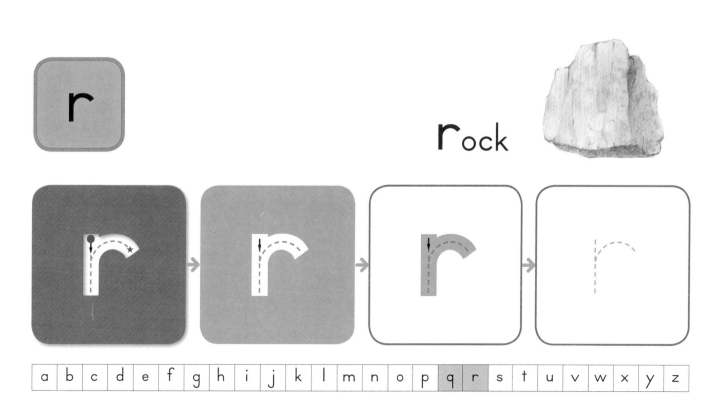

rock

| a | b | c | d | e | f | g | h | i | j | k | l | m | n | o | p | q | r | s | t | u | v | w | x | y | z |

Writing **s** and **t**

■ Trace the letters.

S

Sand

t

tree

| a | b | c | d | e | f | g | h | i | j | k | l | m | n | o | p | q | r | s | t | u | v | w | x | y | z |

■ Trace the letters.

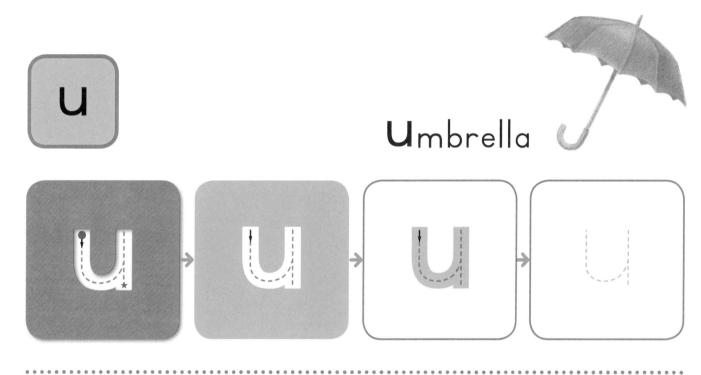

Umbrella

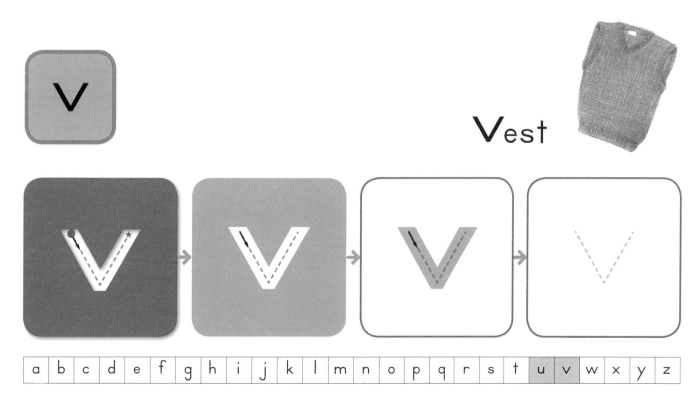

Vest

| a | b | c | d | e | f | g | h | i | j | k | l | m | n | o | p | q | r | s | t | u | v | w | x | y | z |

Writing **w** and **x**

■ Trace the letters.

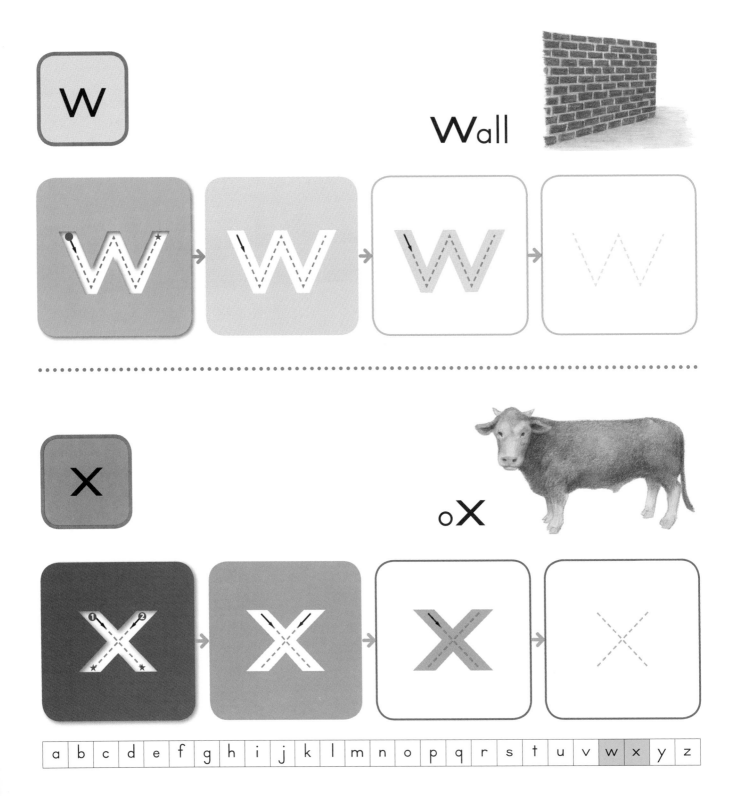

W

Wall

x

oX

■ Trace the letters.

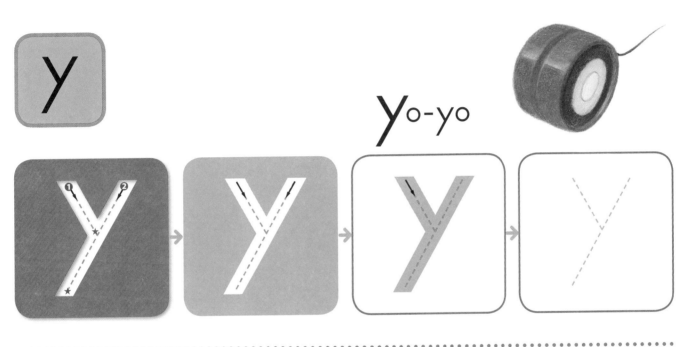

Yo-yo

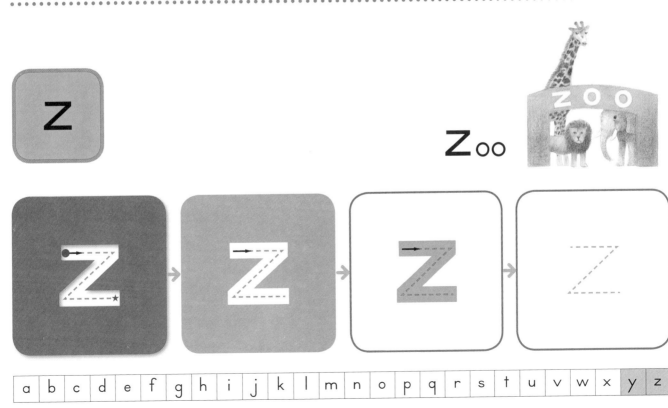

Zoo

a	b	c	d	e	f	g	h	i	j	k	l	m	n	o	p	q	r	s	t	u	v	w	x	y	z

Review **a** to **z**

■ Trace the letters in the table below.

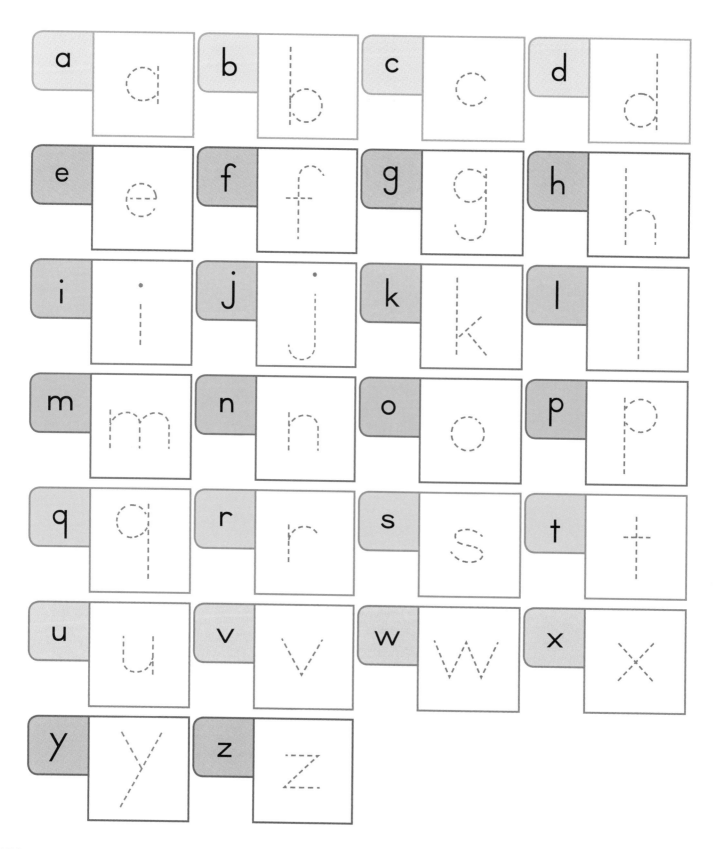

Writing Words
'a' Sound

To parents On the following pages, your child will practice tracing words in rhyming pairs. By repeating rhyming words with the short "a" vowel sound, your child will gain an awareness of the connection between letters and the sounds they represent.

■ Say each letter aloud as you trace it. Then try to say the word aloud. Pay special attention to the letters in color.

■ Say each letter aloud as you trace it. Then try to say the word aloud. Pay special attention to the letters in color.

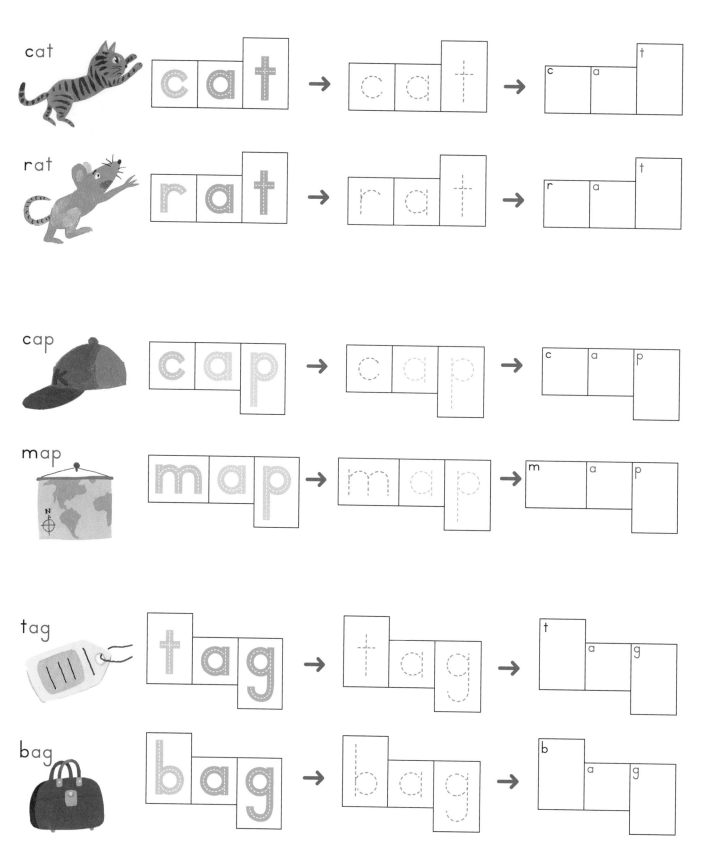

cat

rat

cap

map

tag

bag

Writing Words

'e' Sound

Name

Date

To parents Please help your child to say the sound of the individual letters as he or she traces them. Children should not be forced to blend the letters or sound out the words until they are ready. Try to allow your child to demonstrate their skills naturally, so that they develop positive feelings about learning independently.

■ Say each letter aloud as you trace it. Then try to say the word aloud. Pay special attention to the letters in color.

■ Say each letter aloud as you trace it. Then try to say the word aloud. Pay special attention to the letters in color.

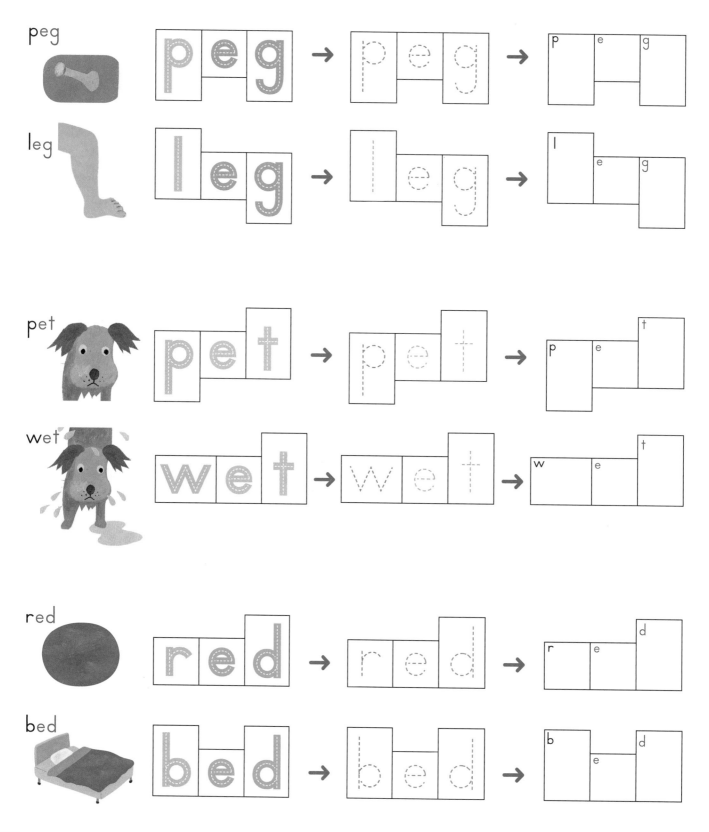

peg

leg

pet

wet

red

bed

27 Writing Words
'i' Sound

Name

Date

To parents If your child is having trouble completing the exercises on these pages, try our other workbooks, such as *My Book of RHYMING WORDS* or *My Book of RHYMING WORDS & PHRASES*, for more practice.

■ Say each letter aloud as you trace it. Then try to say the word aloud. Pay special attention to the letters in color.

■ Say each letter aloud as you trace it. Then try to say the word aloud. Pay special attention to the letters in color.

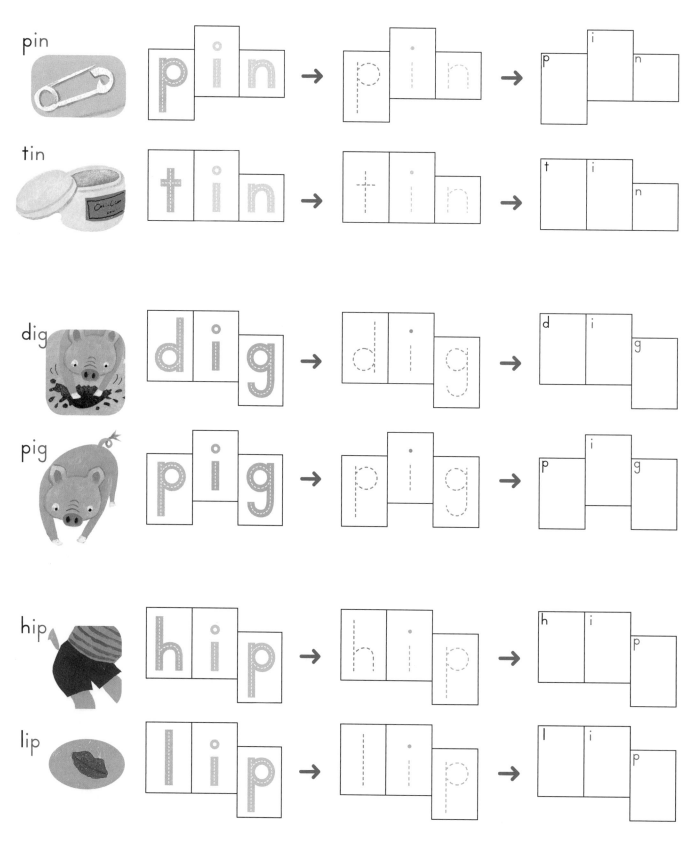

pin

tin

dig

pig

hip

lip

Writing Words
'o' Sound

Name

....

Date

To parents Writing words can be a difficult exercise for young children. Be sure to give your child plenty of encouragement and praise for their hard work.

■ Say each letter aloud as you trace it. Then try to say the word aloud. Pay special attention to the letters in color.

■ Say each letter aloud as you trace it. Then try to say the word aloud. Pay special attention to the letters in color.

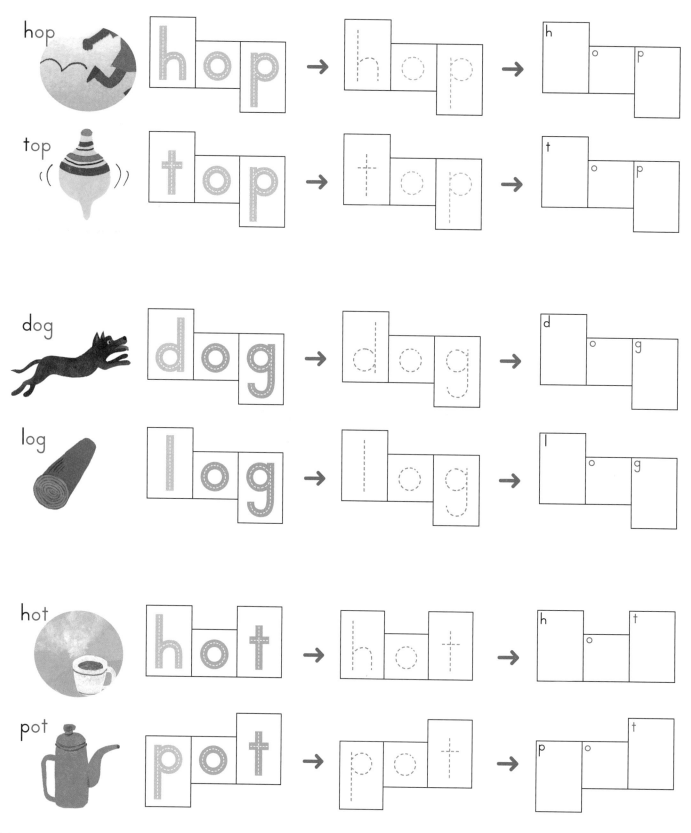

hop

top

dog

log

hot

pot

■ Say each letter aloud as you trace it. Then try to say the word aloud. Pay special attention to the letters in color.

sun

cup

run

pup

rug

bug

■ Say each letter aloud as you trace it. Then try to say the word aloud.
Pay special attention to the letters in color.

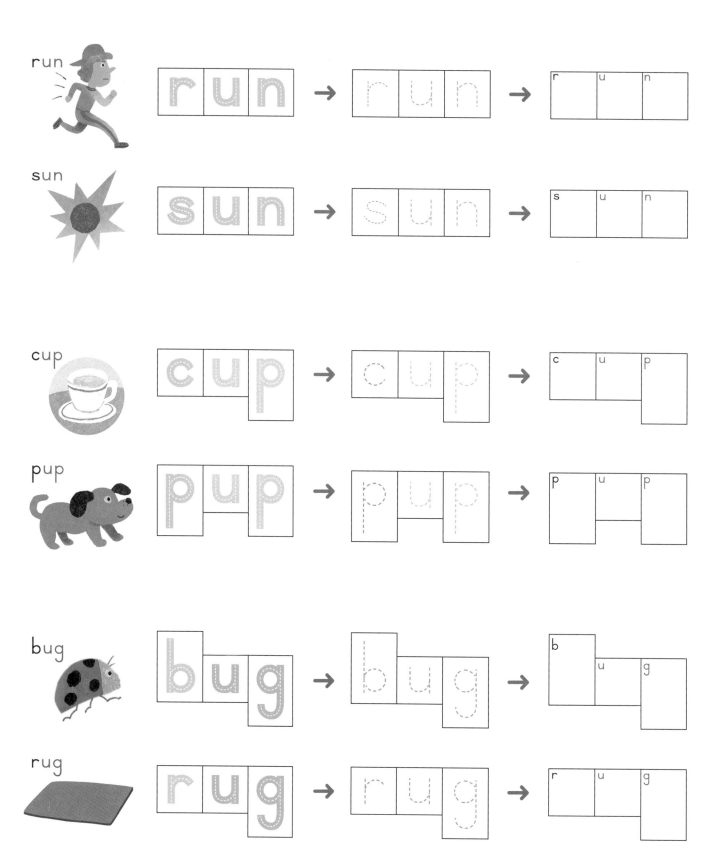

run

sun

cup

pup

bug

rug

To parents This page is an opportunity for you to see how much more practice your child may need in this subject. No matter how well your child does, remember to praise them for their effort.

■ Write the uppercase letters in the table below.

A	B	C	D	E	F
G	H	I	J	K	L
M	N	O	P	Q	R
S	T	U	V	W	X
Y	Z				

Review
Lowercase Letters

■ Write the lowercase letters in the table below.

a	b	c	d	e	f
g	h	i	j	k	l
m	n	o	p	q	r
s	t	u	v	w	x
y	z				

Review
Rhyming Words

Name

Date

To parents Do not be concerned with your child's results on these review pages. Typically, your child will be working on these concepts in kindergarten and this practice will serve as good preparation for that work. Remember to encourage your child for his or her hard work.

■ Write the words below. Use the pictures and letters as hints.

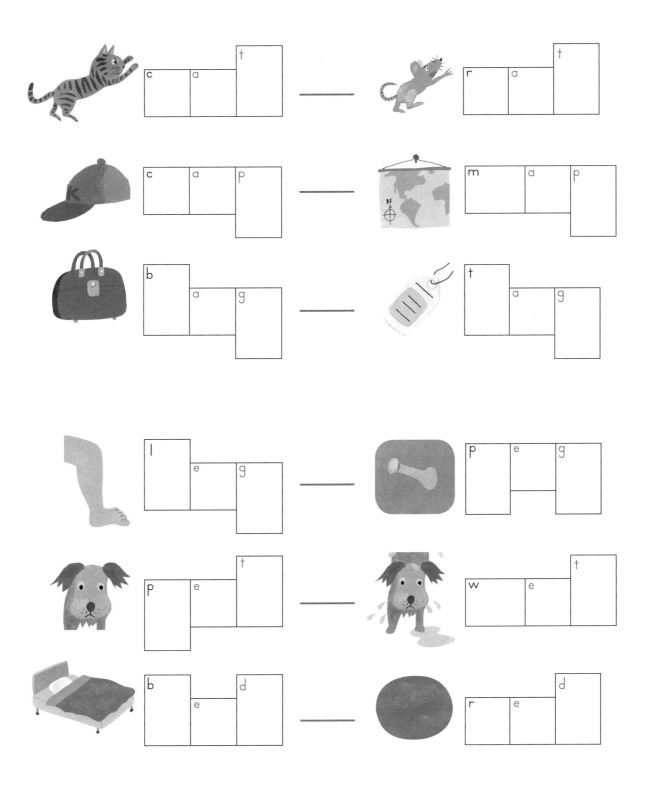

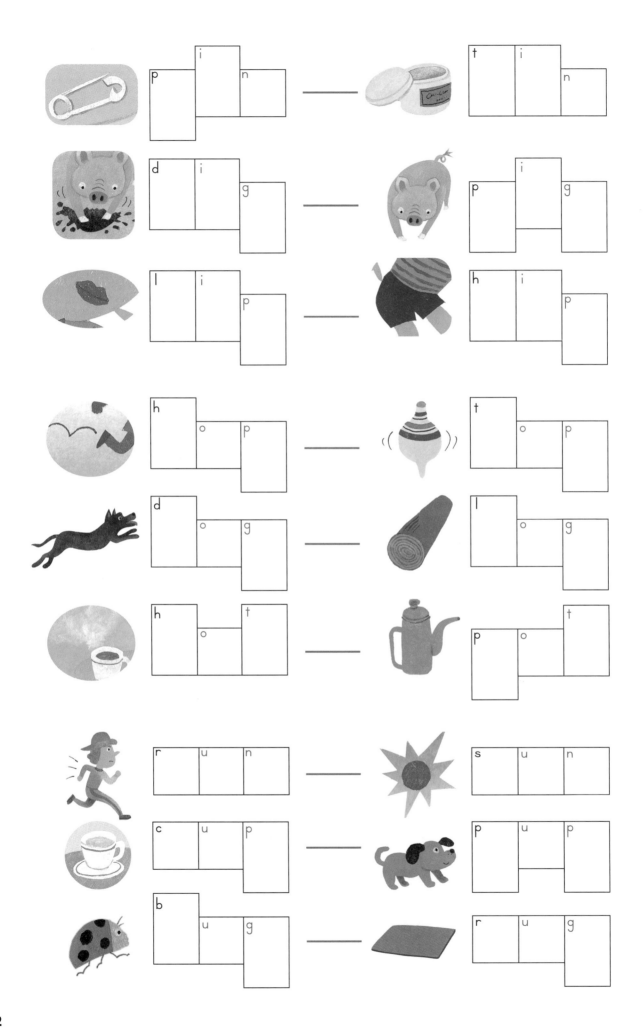

| | p | i | | | | t | i | |
| | | | n | | | | | n |

| | d | i | | | | | i | |
| | | | g | | p | | | g |

| | l | i | | | | h | i | |
| | | | p | | | | | p |

| | h | | | | | t | | |
| | | o | p | | | | o | p |

| | d | | | | | l | | |
| | | o | g | | | | o | g |

| | h | | t | | | | | t |
| | | o | | | | p | o | |

| r | u | n | | | s | u | n |

| c | u | p | | | p | u | p |

| b | | | | | r | u | g |
| | u | g | | | | | |

Are You Ready for Kindergarten?

Math Skills

5

Table of Contents

To parents: Math Skills

In this section your child will complete activities designed to prepare him or her for early number and math skills. By practicing each of the math skills taught in this section, your child will be ready for academic success in kindergarten.

First, your child will learn numbers 1-30, then he or she will practice writing those numbers, and finally your child will work on counting and ordering those numbers. In the last portion of the section, your child will work on patterns, shapes, and following instructions. Each topic is presented in Kumon's step-by-step method to allow your child to learn math skills without frustration.

This skill will take plenty of practice to master. If your child struggles with any particular part of this section, please refer to the appropriate book from our other preschool products for more focused work.

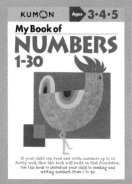

My Book of
NUMBERS 1-30

My Book of
NUMBER GAMES 1-70

Kumon Flash Cards
NUMBERS 1-30
WRITE AND WIPE

Kumon Flash Cards
SHAPES
WRITE AND WIPE

How to hold a pencil properly

There are several ways to teach children to hold a pencil properly. Here is one example.

It can be difficult for a child who does not yet have enough strength in his or her hand and fingers to hold the pencil properly. Please teach this skill gradually, so that your child will remain interested and willing to hold a pencil naturally.

Help your child form an "L" shape with his or her thumb and forefinger as pictured here. Place the pencil against the top of the bent middle finger and on the thumb joint.

Now, have your child squeeze the pencil with the thumb and forefinger.

Check the way that your child is holding the pencil against the picture to help decide whether or not it is the proper way.

Counting Numbers
1 to 5

Name

....

Date

To parents Write your child's name and date in the boxes above. Teach your child the order of numbers from 1 to 5 by saying the numbers aloud with him or her at first.

■ Draw a line from ① to ⑤ in order while saying each number aloud.

| 1 | 2 | 3 | 4 | 5 |

■ Draw a line from ① to ⑤ in order while saying each number aloud.

| 1 | 2 | 3 | 4 | 5 |

Counting Numbers
1 to 10

Name

Date

■ Draw a line from ① to ⑩ in order while saying each number aloud.

| 1 | 2 | 3 | 4 | 5 | 6 | 7 | 8 | 9 | 10 |

■ Draw a line from ① to ⑩ in order while saying each number aloud.

1 2 3 4 5 6 7 8 9 10

198

■ Draw a line from ① to ⑮ in order while saying each number aloud.

| 1 | 2 | 3 | 4 | 5 | 6 | 7 | 8 | 9 | 10 | 11 | 12 | 13 | 14 | 15 |

■ Draw a line from ① to ⑮ in order while saying each number aloud.

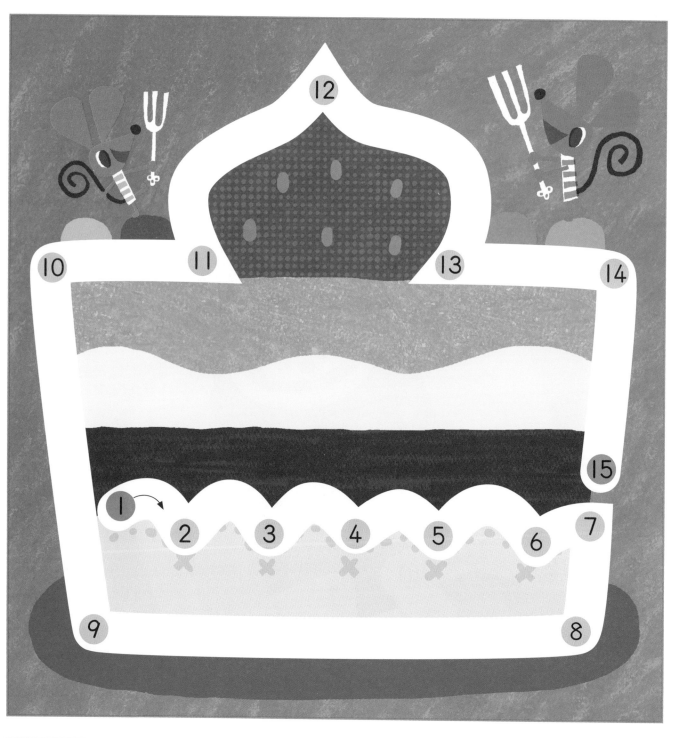

| I | 2 | 3 | 4 | 5 | 6 | 7 | 8 | 9 | I0 | II | I2 | I3 | I4 | I5 |

Counting Numbers
1 to 20

Name

Date

■ Draw a line from ① to ⑳ in order while saying each number aloud.

| 1 | 2 | 3 | 4 | 5 | 6 | 7 | 8 | 9 | 10 | 11 | 12 | 13 | 14 | 15 | 16 | 17 | 18 | 19 | 20 |

■ Draw a line from ① to ⑳ in order while saying each number aloud.

| 1 | 2 | 3 | 4 | 5 | 6 | 7 | 8 | 9 | 10 | 11 | 12 | 13 | 14 | 15 | 16 | 17 | 18 | 19 | 20 |

Counting Numbers
1 to 25

Name

Date

To parents Your child's lines may not be steady at first, but they should improve with practice. Make sure to praise your child for his or her hard work.

■ Draw a line from ① to ㉕ in order while saying each number aloud.

| 1 | 2 | 3 | 4 | 5 | 6 | 7 | 8 | 9 | 10 | 11 | 12 | 13 | 14 | 15 | 16 | 17 | 18 | 19 | 20 | 21 | 22 | 23 | 24 | 25 |

■ Draw a line from ① to ㉕ in order while saying each number aloud.

| 1 | 2 | 3 | 4 | 5 | 6 | 7 | 8 | 9 | 10 | 11 | 12 | 13 | 14 | 15 | 16 | 17 | 18 | 19 | 20 | 21 | 22 | 23 | 24 | 25 |

■ Draw a line from ① to ㉚ in order while saying each number aloud.

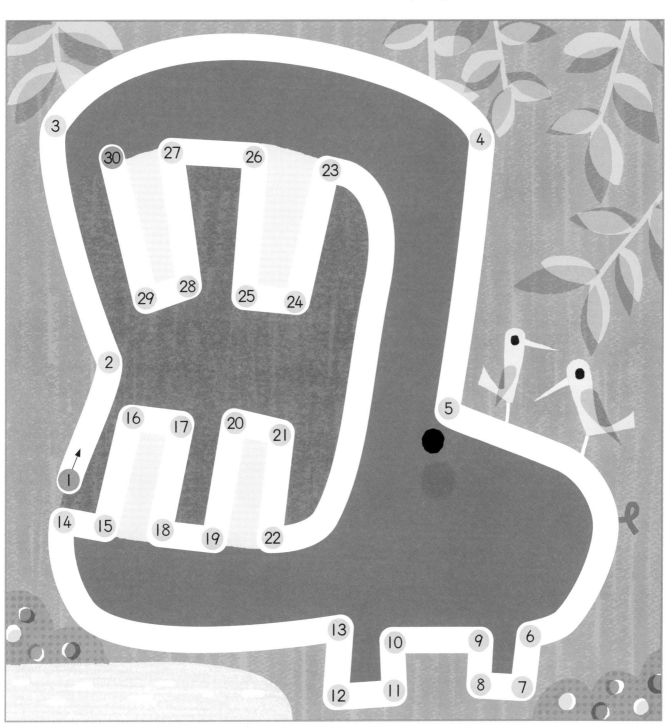

| 1 | 2 | 3 | 4 | 5 | 6 | 7 | 8 | 9 | 10 | 11 | 12 | 13 | 14 | 15 | 16 | 17 | 18 | 19 | 20 | 21 | 22 | 23 | 24 | 25 | 26 | 27 | 28 | 29 | 30 |

Draw a line from ① to ㉚ in order while saying each number aloud.

| 1 | 2 | 3 | 4 | 5 | 6 | 7 | 8 | 9 | 10 | 11 | 12 | 13 | 14 | 15 | 16 | 17 | 18 | 19 | 20 | 21 | 22 | 23 | 24 | 25 | 26 | 27 | 28 | 29 | 30 |

Counting Numbers
1 to 10

Name

....

Date

To parents   For additional fun, ask your child to guess what is in the picture before he or she connects the dots. Once your child is done, they can also color in the object they have created!

■ Draw a line from 1 to 10 in order while saying each number aloud.

| 1 | 2 | 3 | 4 | 5 | 6 | 7 | 8 | 9 | 10 |

(tree) **207**

1 to 15

■ Draw a line from 1 to 15 in order while saying each number aloud.

| 1 | 2 | 3 | 4 | 5 | 6 | 7 | 8 | 9 | 10 | 11 | 12 | 13 | 14 | 15 |

(ship)

Counting Numbers
1 to 20

Name

Date

To parents   Remember to encourage your child as the exercises get more challenging. If your child has difficulty finding the next number, please point it out for him or her. The object is to practice counting numbers and to enjoy the process.

■ Draw a line from 1 to 20 in order while saying each number aloud.

| 1 | 2 | 3 | 4 | 5 | 6 | 7 | 8 | 9 | 10 | 11 | 12 | 13 | 14 | 15 | 16 | 17 | 18 | 19 | 20 |

1 to 25

■ Draw a line from 1 to 25 in order while saying each number aloud.

| 1 | 2 | 3 | 4 | 5 | 6 | 7 | 8 | 9 | 10 | 11 | 12 | 13 | 14 | 15 | 16 | 17 | 18 | 19 | 20 | 21 | 22 | 23 | 24 | 25 |

(hippo)

Counting Numbers
1 to 30

Name
....
Date

To parents If these exercises are becoming too difficult for your child, try *My Book of NUMBERS 1-30* or *My Book of NUMBER GAMES 1-70* for more practice.

■ Draw a line from 1 to 30 in order while saying each number aloud.

1	2	3	4	5	6	7	8	9	10	11	12	13	14	15	16	17	18	19	20	21	22	23	24	25	26	27	28	29	30

1 to **30**

■ Draw a line from 1 to 30 in order while saying each number aloud.

| 1 | 2 | 3 | 4 | 5 | 6 | 7 | 8 | 9 | 10 | 11 | 12 | 13 | 14 | 15 | 16 | 17 | 18 | 19 | 20 | 21 | 22 | 23 | 24 | 25 | 26 | 27 | 28 | 29 | 30 |

(crocodile)

Writing Numbers
1 and **2**

Name
Date

To parents Now your child will practice tracing the numbers one through ten. Though the stroke path on this page is wide, it may be challenging for your child to draw straight lines. It is more important that your child enjoy learning than it is for him or her to correctly write these numbers. Praise your child's efforts no matter the results.

■ Write the number 1 and say it aloud.

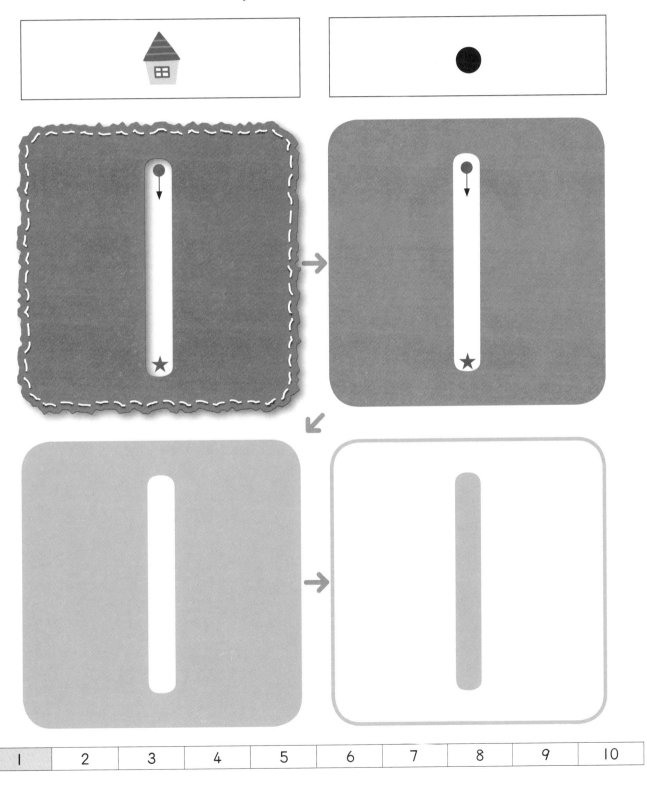

1	2	3	4	5	6	7	8	9	10

Write the number 2 and say it aloud.

Writing Numbers
3 and **4**

Name

Date

■ Write the number 3 and say it aloud.

Write the number 4 and say it aloud.

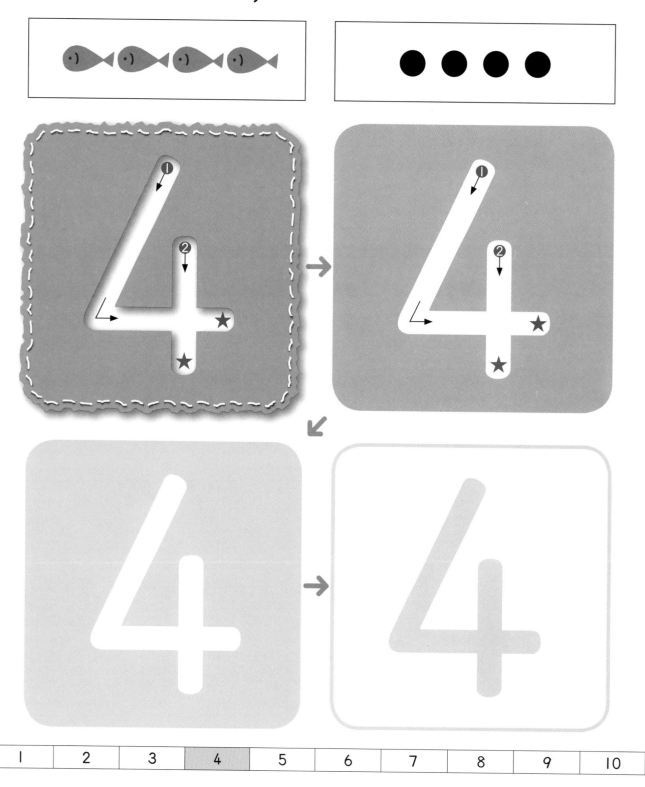

| 1 | 2 | 3 | 4 | 5 | 6 | 7 | 8 | 9 | 10 |

Writing Numbers
5 and 6

Name
....
Date

To parents Five is a difficult number to write. Try helping your child trace the first example, or try pointing out the stroke order, so that your child has a little help the first time he or she attempts to write the number.

■ Write the number 5 and say it aloud.

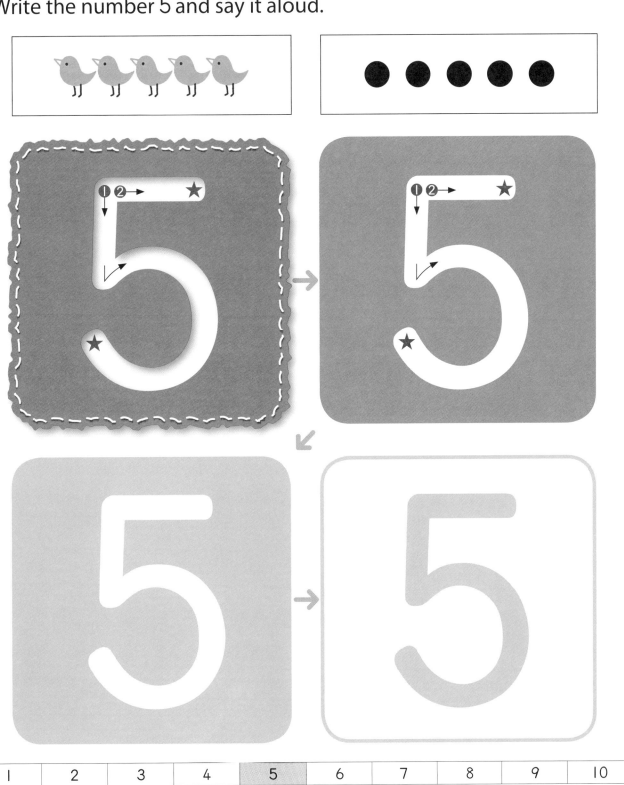

Write the number 6 and say it aloud.

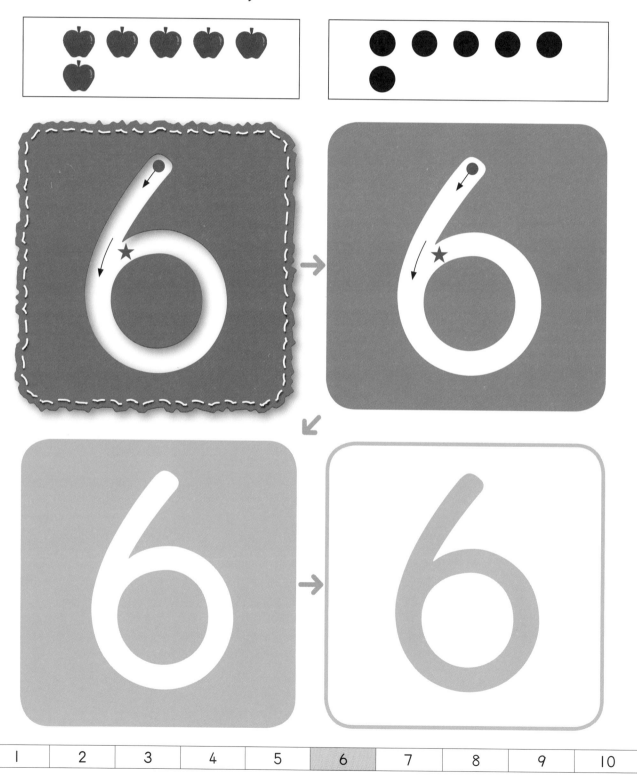

Writing Numbers
7 and 8

■ Write the number 7 and say it aloud.

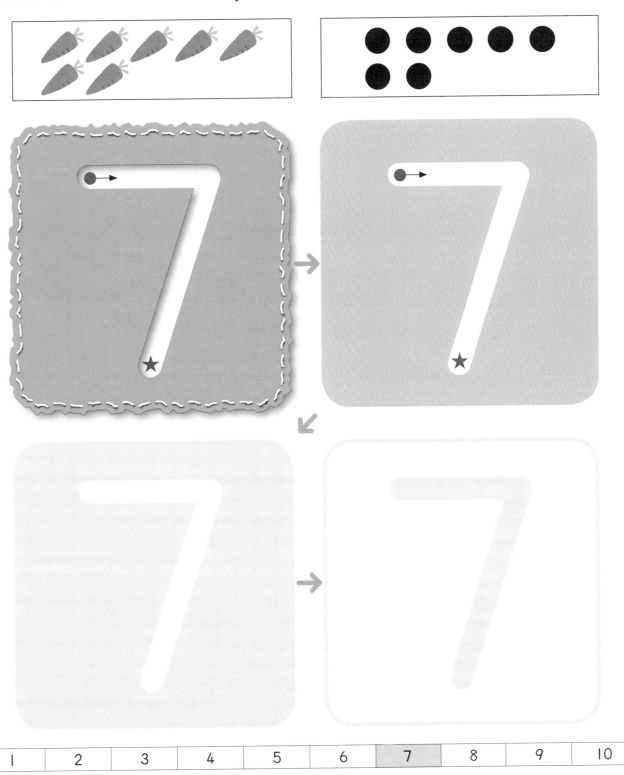

1	2	3	4	5	6	7	8	9	10

Write the number 8 and say it aloud.

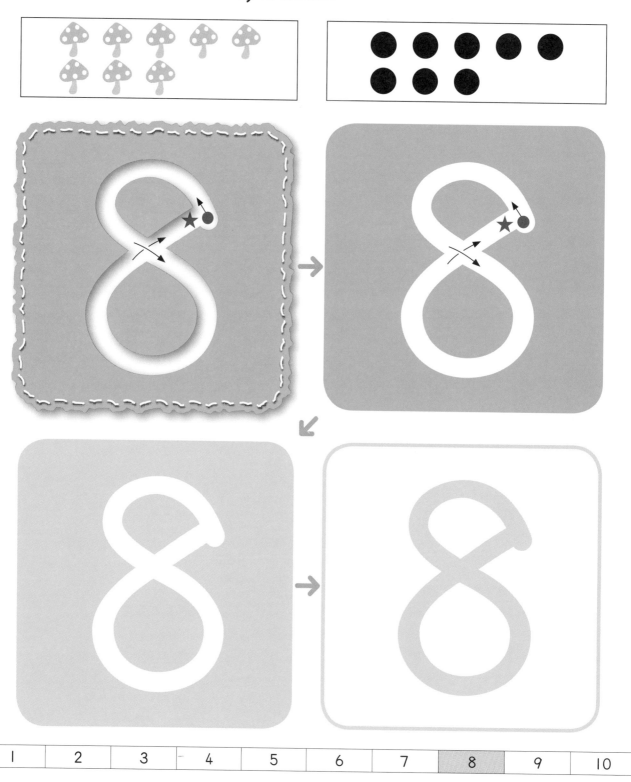

Writing Numbers
9 and 10

Name

....

Date

To parents Try helping your child practice counting on a daily basis. Find opportunities to have fun with numbers at the grocery store, in the park, or wherever you are.

■ Write the number *9* and say it aloud.

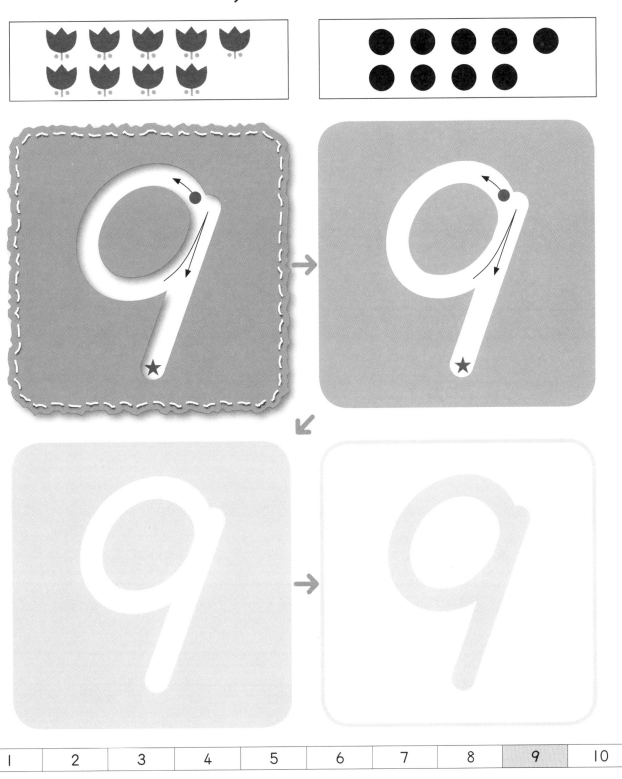

| 1 | 2 | 3 | 4 | 5 | 6 | 7 | 8 | 9 | 10 |

■ Write the number 10 and say it aloud.

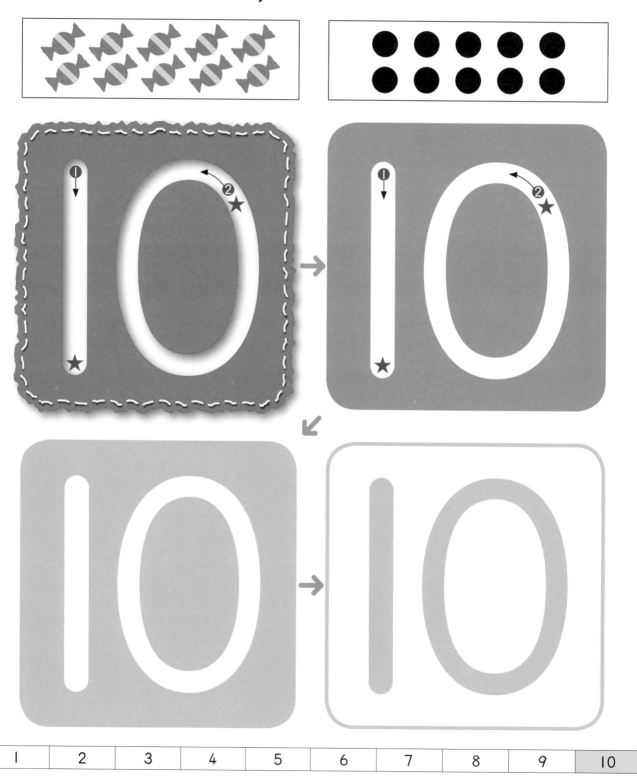

| 1 | 2 | 3 | 4 | 5 | 6 | 7 | 8 | 9 | 10 |

How Many?
1 to 10

Name

Date

To parents Now that there is no stroke order shown, and the space is narrower, your child may encounter some difficulty. If your child struggles to write in the provided space, try *My Book of NUMBERS 1-30* for more practice.

■ How many are there? Trace the numbers and fill the empty boxes.

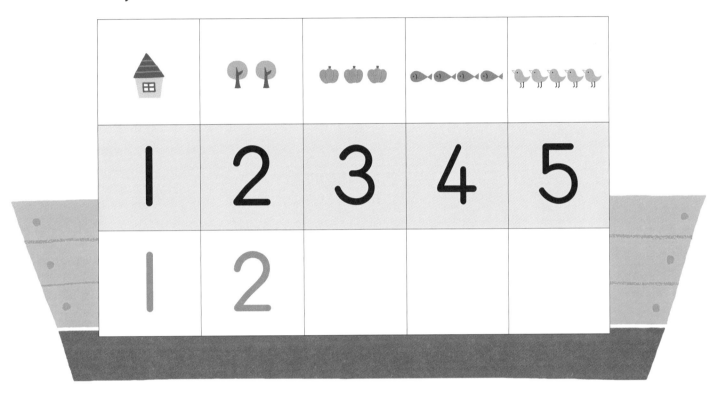

How many are there? Trace the numbers and fill the empty boxes.

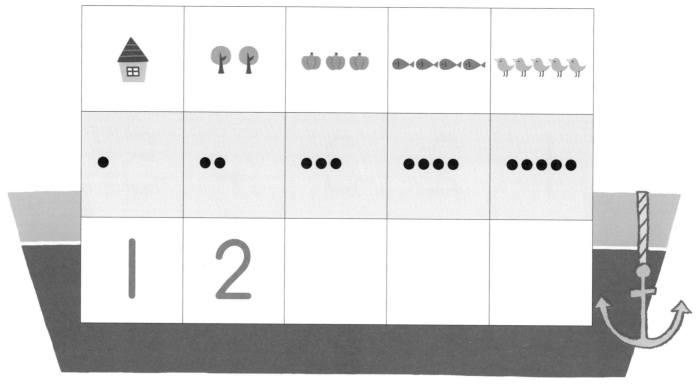

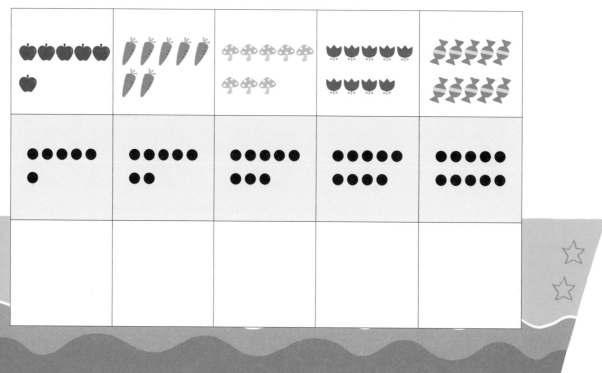

■ How many are there? Trace and write the numbers.

| 1 1 | 1 2 | 1 3 | 1 4 | 1 5 |

■ Trace the numbers. Then fill in the missing numbers. Say each number aloud.

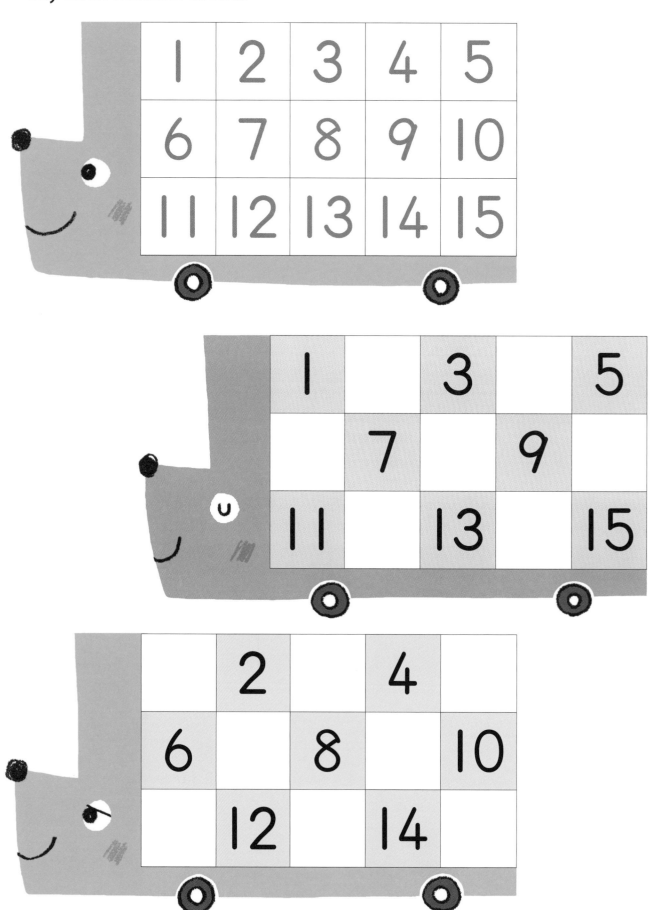

1	2	3	4	5
6	7	8	9	10
11	12	13	14	15

1		3		5
	7		9	
11		13		15

	2		4	
6		8		10
	12		14	

How Many?
1 to 20

Name

Date

■ How many are there? Trace and write the numbers.

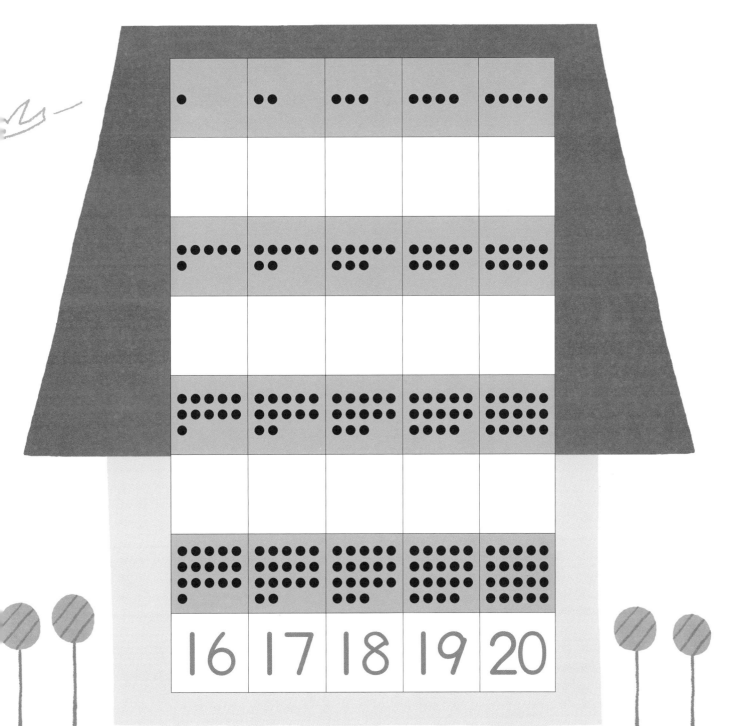

■ Trace the numbers. Then fill in the missing numbers.
  Say each number aloud.

1	2	3	4	5
6	7	8	9	10
11	12	13	14	15
16	17	18	19	20

1		3		5
	7		9	
11		13		15
	17		19	

18 How Many?
1 to 25

How many are there? Trace and write the numbers.

21 22 23 24 25

■ Trace the numbers. Then fill in the missing numbers.
  Say each number aloud.

1	2	3	4	5
6	7	8	9	10
11	12	13	14	15
16	17	18	19	20
21	22	23	24	25

	2		4	
6		8		10
	12		14	
16		18		20
	22		24	

230

How Many?
1 to 30

Name

....

Date

To parents   The numbers up to 30 are considered the kindergarten standard in most places. If your child is able to complete these pages, he or she is more than ready for kindergarten. More probably, your child has benefitted from the practice and will be prepared to see similar exercises when he or she attends the first day at kindergarten.

■ How many are there? Trace and write the numbers.

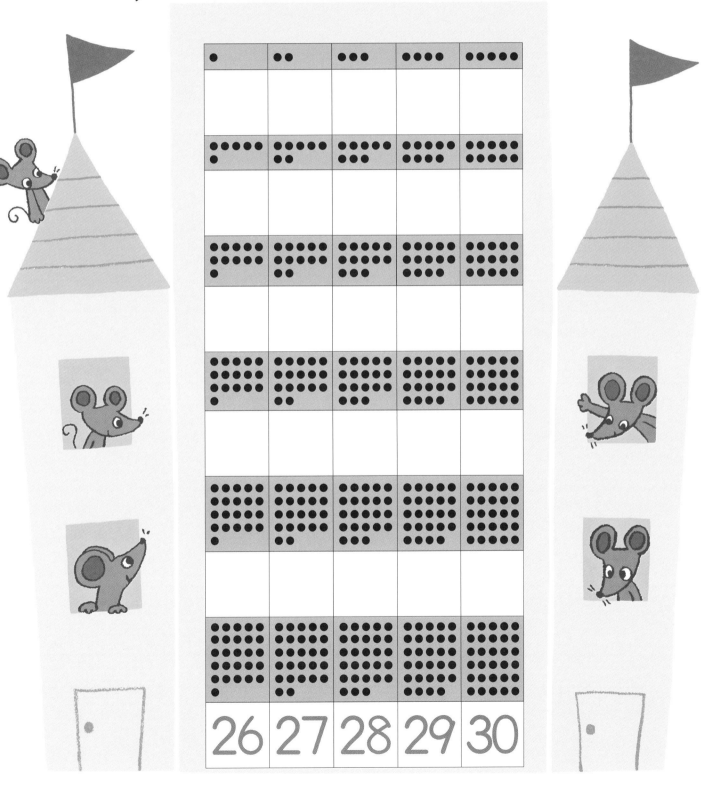

■ Trace the numbers. Then fill in the missing numbers.
Say each number aloud.

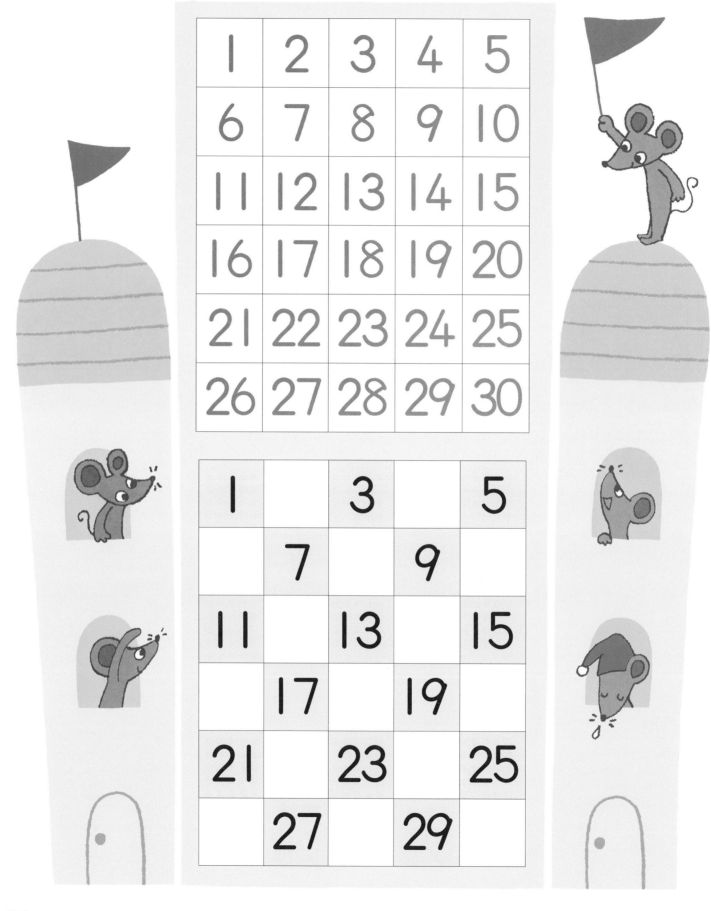

1	2	3	4	5
6	7	8	9	10
11	12	13	14	15
16	17	18	19	20
21	22	23	24	25
26	27	28	29	30

1		3		5
	7		9	
11		13		15
	17		19	
21		23		25
	27		29	

Counting Numbers
1 to 30

Name

Date

■ Fill in the missing numbers. Say each number aloud.

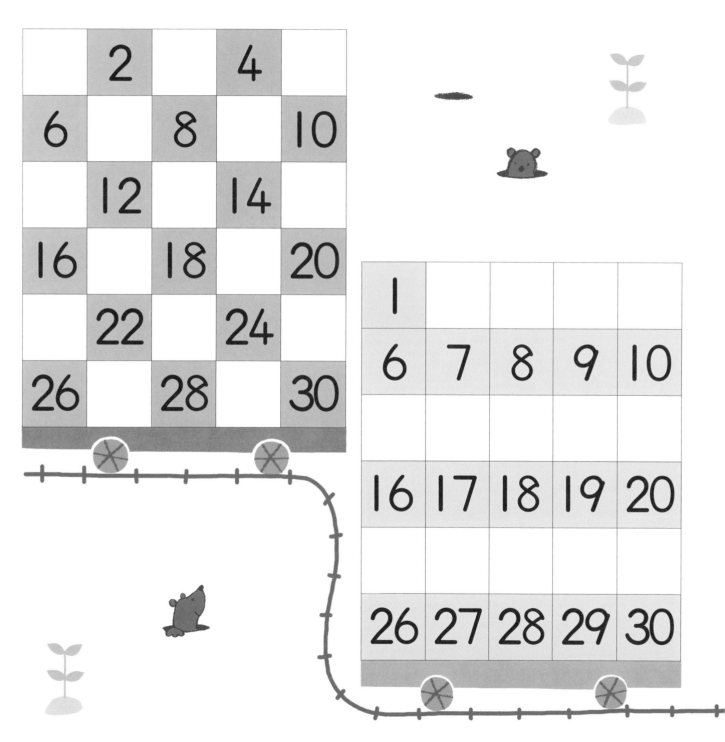

	2		4	
6		8		10
	12		14	
16		18		20
	22		24	
26		28		30

1				
6	7	8	9	10
16	17	18	19	20
26	27	28	29	30

■ Fill in the missing numbers. Say each number aloud.

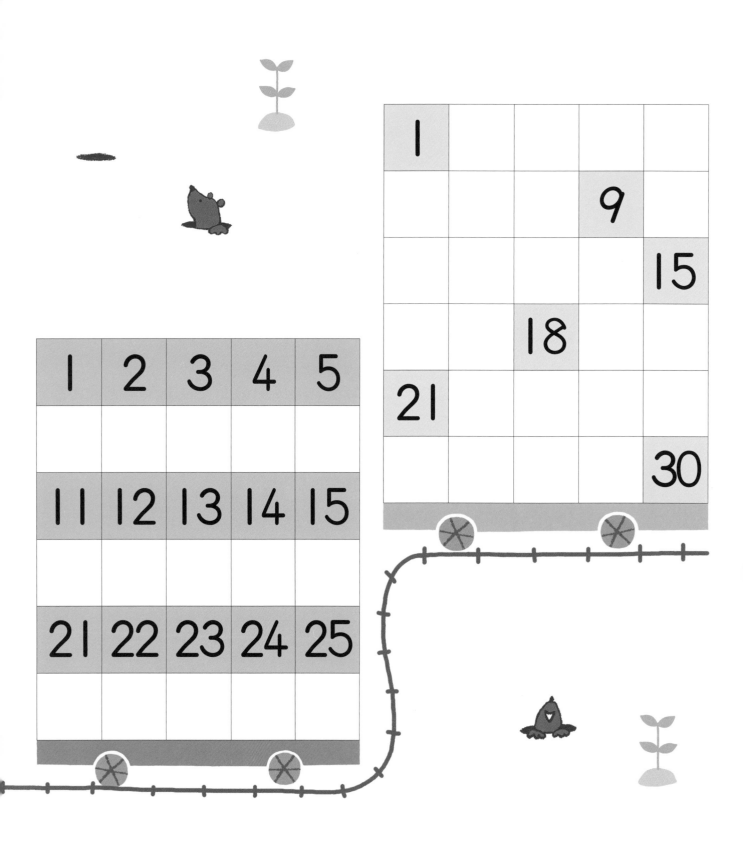

1	2	3	4	5
11	12	13	14	15
21	22	23	24	25

1				
			9	
				15
		18		
21				
				30

Drawing Shapes
Circle

Name

Date

To parents The following pages will give your child the chance to refine his or her motor control skills while learning the names of common shapes. Try pointing out shapes in the world around your child, as this will help him or her remember their names.

■ Draw the shapes below.

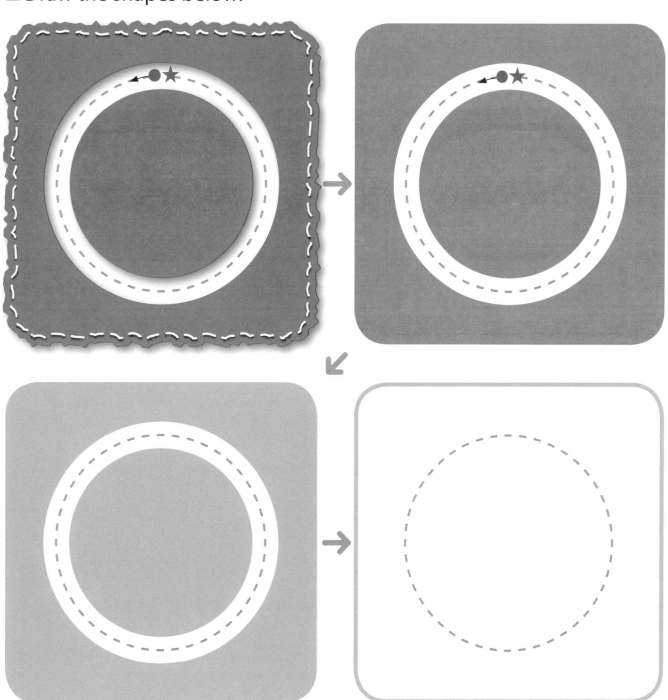

Oval

■ Draw the shapes below.

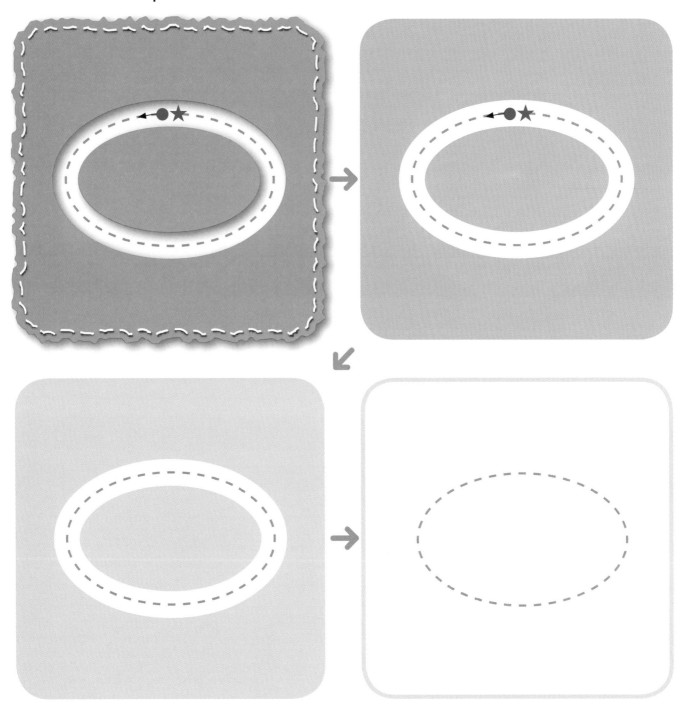

Drawing Shapes
Square

Name

Date

To parents   In order to help your child understand what makes a square, you could point out the characteristics of the shape. Show your child that a square has four equal, straight sides, for example.

■ Draw the shapes below.

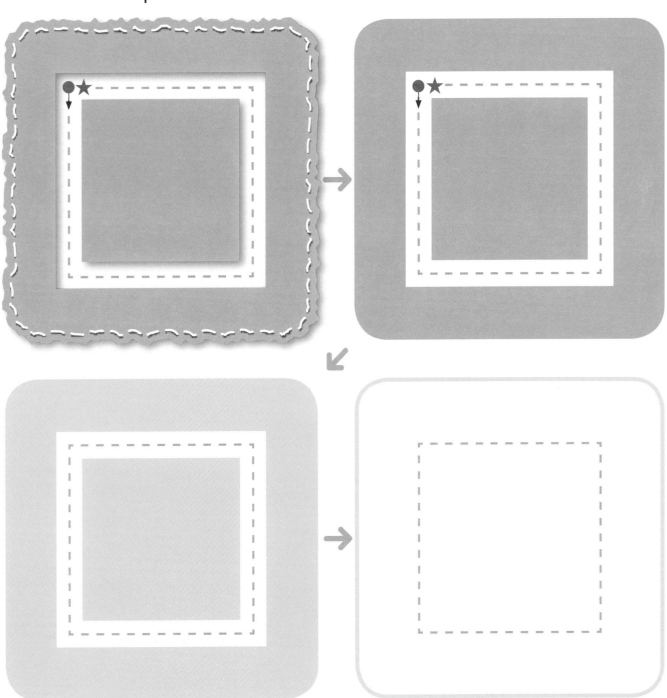

Rectangle

■ Draw the shapes below.

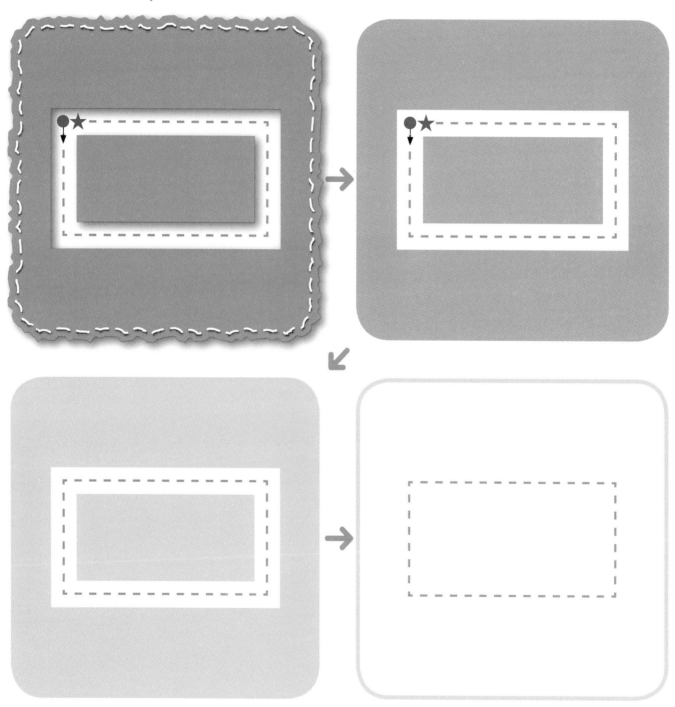

Drawing Shapes
Triangle

Name

Date

■ Draw the shapes below.

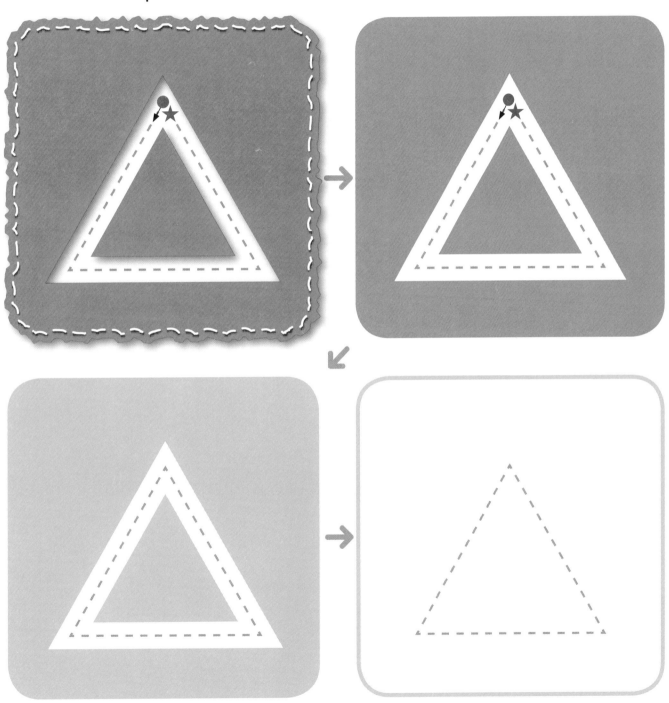

Diamond （Rhombus）

■ Draw the shapes below.

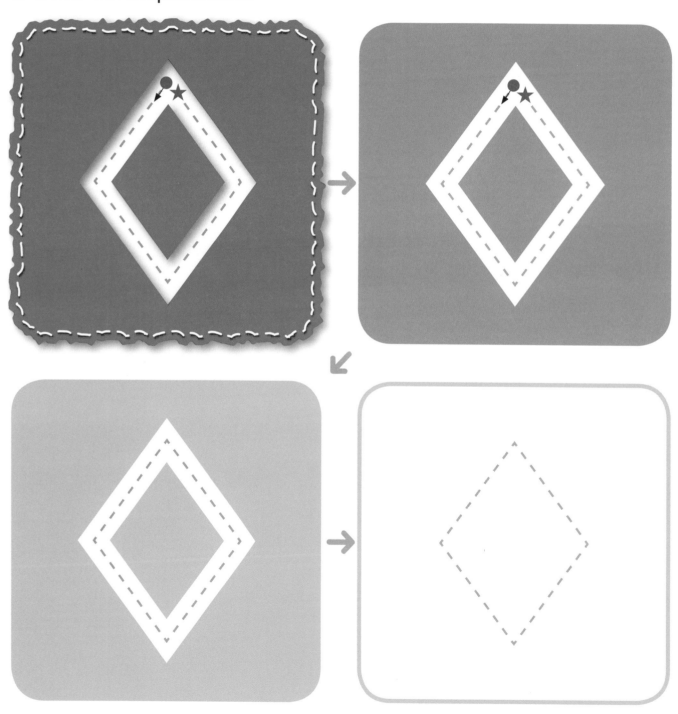

Which is the Same Shape?

Date

To parents   This page will help your child spot similarities in shapes of different sizes. If your child struggles to find the correct shape, try pointing out the characteristics of the shape you are looking for. For example, a circle is perfectly round – what other shapes on this page are perfectly round?

■ Circle the shapes below that are the same shape as the sample.

sample

circle

■ Circle the shapes below that are the same shape as the sample.

sample

square

Which is the Same Shape?

Name

....

Date

■ Circle the shapes below that are the same shape as the sample.

sample

triangle

■ Circle the shapes below that are the same shape as the samples.

sample	sample	sample
oval	rectangle	diamond

Which is the Same Shape and Color?

Name

....

Date

■ Circle the shape below that is the same shape and color as the sample.

sample

red circle

■ Circle the shapes below that are the same shape and color as the samples.

sample

blue square

sample

yellow triangle

Which is the Same Shape and Color?

Name

Date

■ Circle the shapes below that are the same shape and color as the samples.

sample	sample	sample
green circle	purple square	orange diamond

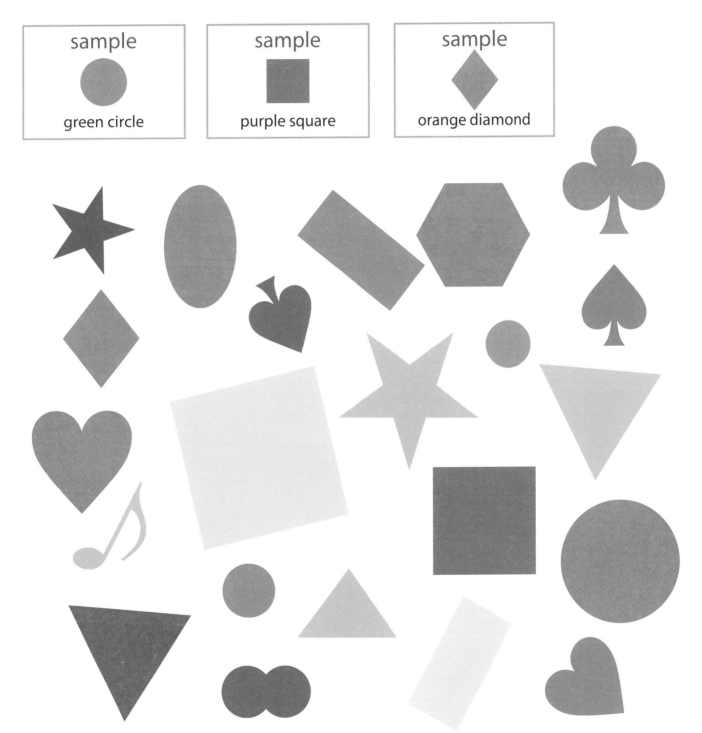

■ Circle the shapes below that are the same shape and color as the samples.

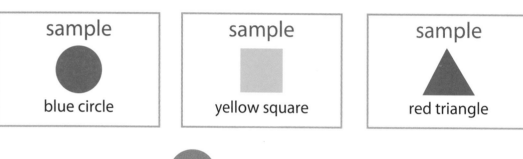

sample

blue circle

sample

yellow square

sample

red triangle

Which is the Same Shape and Color?

■ Find the shapes shown in the samples below.
  Then color them the same color as the sample.

sample

square is orange

sample

rectangle is red

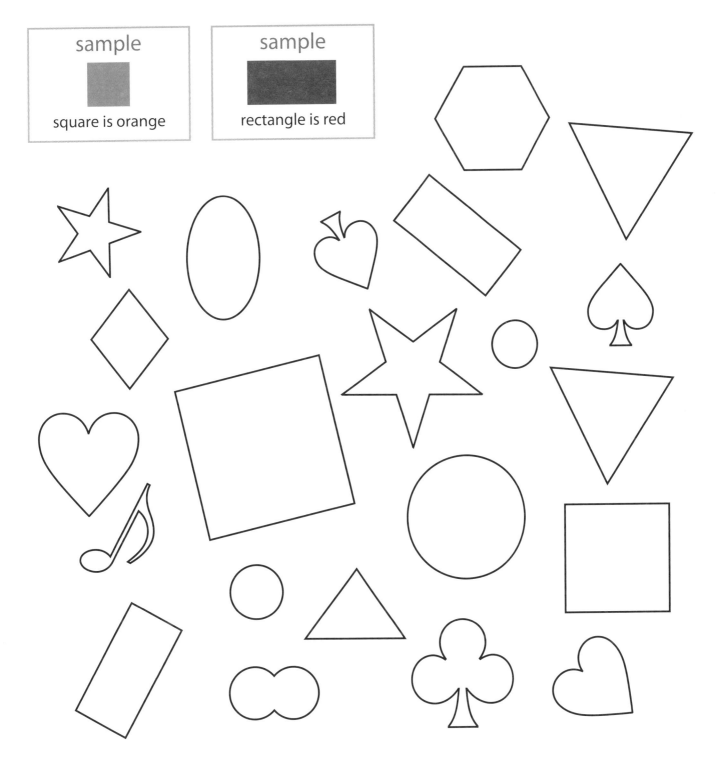

■ Find the shapes shown in the samples below.
  Then color them the same color as the sample.

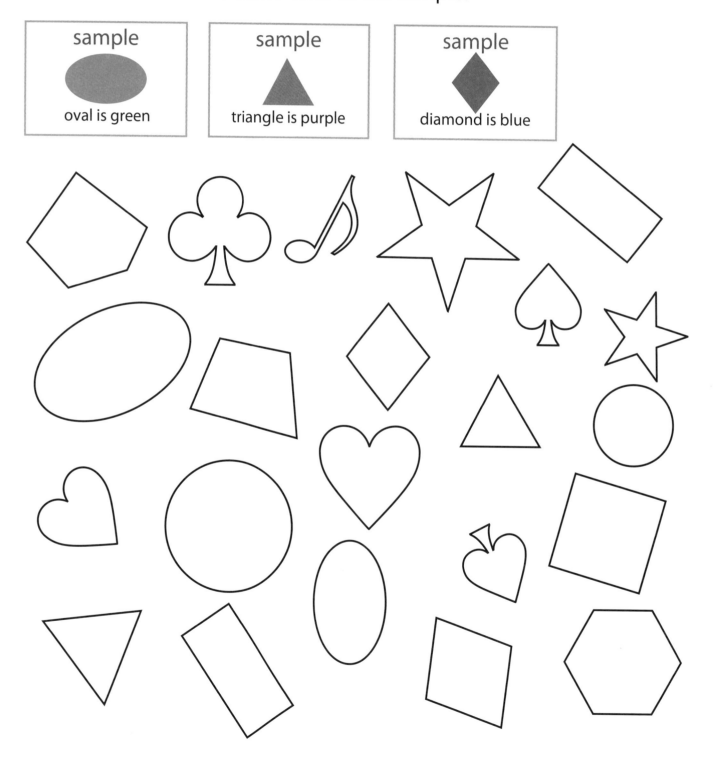

sample	sample	sample
oval is green	triangle is purple	diamond is blue

What is First?
What is Last?

To parents The following pages will help your child follow directions. Please give your child hints if he or she struggles to understand the questions.

■ Circle the first thing in each line below.

Front

Front

Front

■ Color the first thing in each line below.

Front

Front

Front

■ Circle the last thing in each line below.

Front

■ Color the last thing in each line below.

Front

Review

Name

....

Date

To parents Now your child will review some of the concepts he or she has seen in this book. Remember that most of these topics are covered in kindergarten, and that the purpose of this book is to identify what particular skills your child may want to work on. Please see our line of preschool workbooks for further instruction.

■ Draw a line from 1 to 30 in order while saying each number aloud.

(elephant)

How many are there? Write the numbers.

254

Review

Name

....

Date

To parents Remember to congratulate your child for all the work he or she has done. Your child will continue to work on these concepts in kindergarten. Keeping him or her interested and confident is a key part of creating a self-motivated learner!

■ Fill in the missing numbers. Say each number aloud.

1		3		5
6		8		10
11		13		15
16		18		20
21		23		25
26		28		30

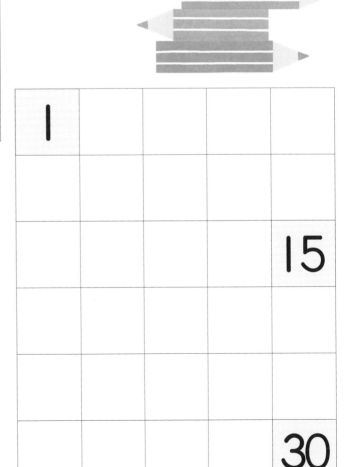

1				
				15
				30

255

■ Find the shapes shown in the samples below.
Then color them the same color as the sample.

sample

circle is
green

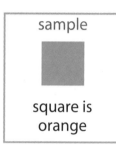

sample

square is
orange

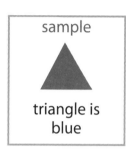

sample

triangle is
blue

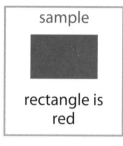

sample

rectangle is
red

sample

diamond is
yellow

Are You Ready for Kindergarten?

Scissor Skills

Table of Contents

To parents: Scissor Skills

In this section your child will complete activities designed to help him or her master scissor control, which develops fine motor control skills. Scissors are one of your child's first tools, and they need not be dangerous if children learn proper scissor control and safety.

First, your child will learn how to hold scissors properly, and to cut one-stroke straight lines. Gradually, your child will cut longer lines, curves, and more intricate shapes as his or her abilities improve. By advancing incrementally, your child will naturally develop finger strength and dexterity, improve scissor control, and enhance his or her understanding of shapes.

Parent Note: The pages in this section are designed to be removed from the book before your child completes them. Please cut the pages out of the workbook before you give them to your child to work on.

This skill will take plenty of practice to master. If your child struggles with any particular part of this section, please refer to the appropriate book from our other preschool products for more focused work.

| My Book of Cutting | Let's Cut Paper! | MORE Let's Cut Paper! | Let's Cut Paper! Amazing Animals | Let's Cut Paper! Food Fun |

How to choose and hold scissors

Scissors can be dangerous if not handled properly. Keep an eye on your child when he or she is using scissors.

＊ Choose safety scissors with round tips.
＊ Choose scissors that suit your child's hands so that he or she can hold them easily.
＊ Choose scissors your child can open and close easily.

Show your child how to put his or her thumb into the smaller hole and his or her forefinger and middle finger into the bigger hole on the scissors. If the bigger hole is large enough, have your child put his or her ring finger into the hole as well.

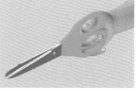

Align your child's hand with the scissors so that they form a straight line when viewed from above. Instruct your child to open the scissors wide and cut half an inch, then open the scissors wide again and cut another half an inch. Repeat this technique. In the beginning, do not be concerned if your child cuts off the line or cannot stop the scissors at a designated point. Observe your child's progress, and encourage him or her to advance one step at a time.

Lion's Mane

To parents Your child will practice cutting short lines with one or two strokes. It is okay if your child goes off the cutting line or cuts unevenly. Please assist your child and keep an eye on him or her to avoid any injuries.

≪ example ≫

■ Cut along ▬▬▬▬. Start from ➡.

259

Sky-High

To parents Your child will practice repeatly opening and closing scissors to cut longer lines. It is okay for your child to stop after one stroke and start over again. When your child has successfully cut each part out, offer lots of praise.

<< example >>

■ Cut along ▬▬▬. Start from ➡.

Connect the Train Cars

≪ example ≫

To parents When your child has completed the cutting, encourage him or her to arrange the parts to make a long train.

■ Cut along ▬▬▬▬ . Start from ▬➡ .

Santa Claus

< example >

To parents The lines on this page are diagonal. Don't be concerned if your child's cutting is uneven. When he or she is finished, you and your child can play with the Santa Claus mask and talk about your favorite winter holidays.

■ Cut along ▬▬▬ . Start from ➡ .

265

Giraffe Family

To parents The lines on this page are longer than earlier exercises. If your child is having difficulty holding the paper steady while cutting, you can place the paper on a table.

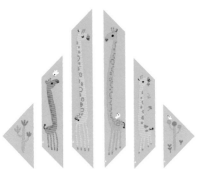

≺ example ≻

■ Cut along ▬▬▬. Start from ➡.

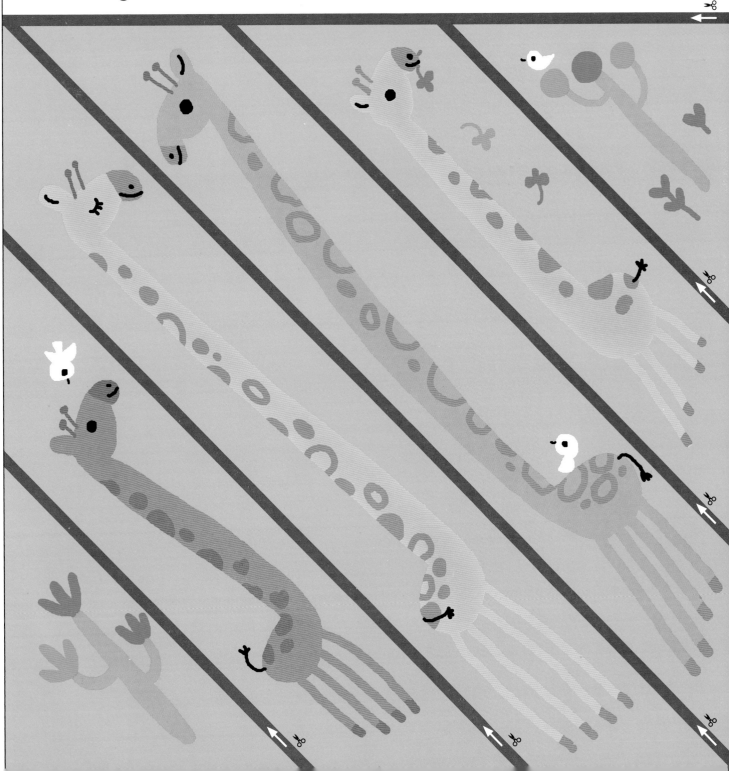

Brush Your Teeth

To parents Your child will practice cutting out the diamond-shaped mirror. When he or she is finished, say "What is in the mirror?"

< example >

■ Cut along ▬▬▬▬. Start from ➡.

269

Over the Rainbow

≺ example ≻

To parents In this exercise, your child will practice cutting curving lines. It is okay if your child goes off the line or cuts in straight lines at first. Help your child open and close the scissors with short strokes in order to cut the curves neatly.

■ Cut along ▬▬▬▬. Start from ➡.

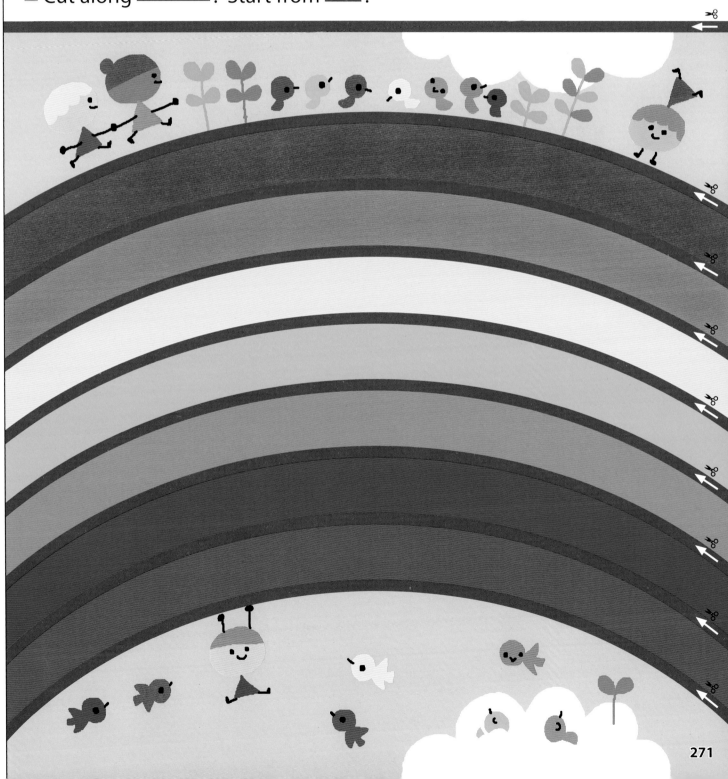

271

Climb a Mountain

To parents On this page, the curving lines are more difficult. Encourage your child to cut curves slowly and steadily. When he or she has successfully cut the paper, offer lots of praise.

‹ example ›

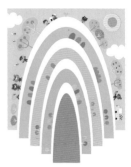

■ Cut along ▬▬▬▬. Start from ▬►.

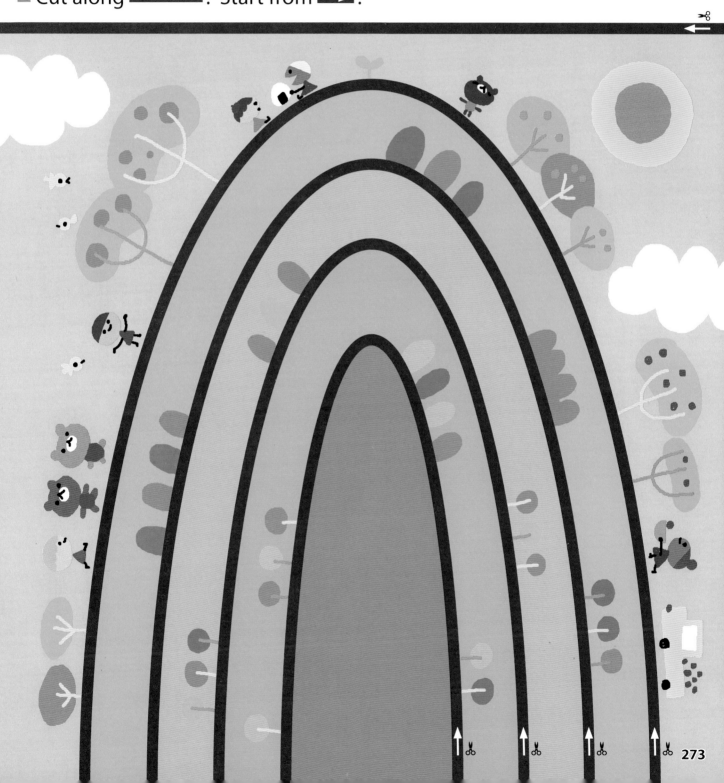

Slice the Cake

« example »

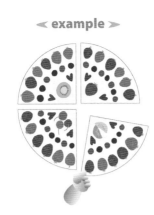

■ Cut along ▬▬▬. Start from ▭➡.

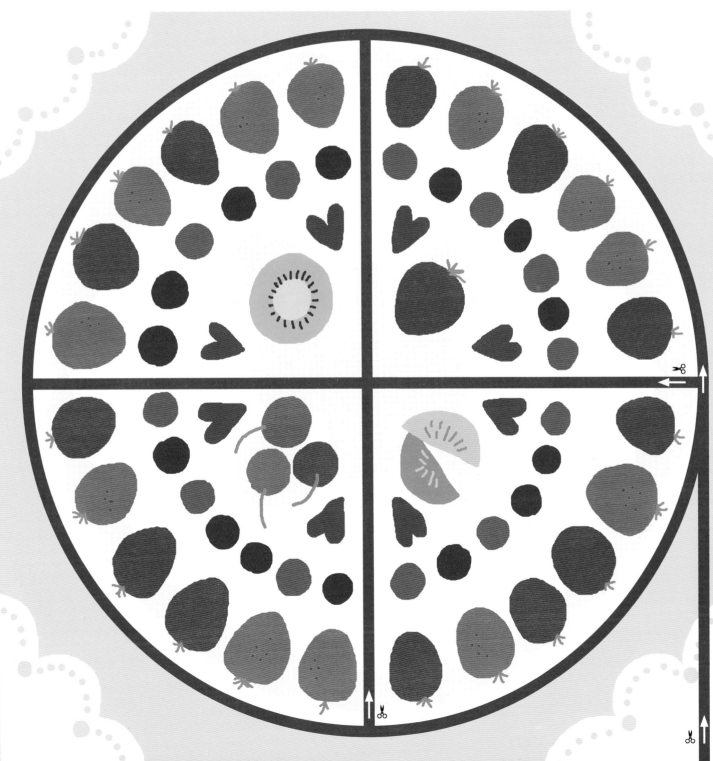

Lobsters

To parents   Cutting in a zigzag is a difficult skill to master. When your child has successfully cut the paper, offer lots of praise. You can also have fun by fighting the lobsters.

‹ example ›

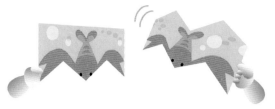

■ Cut along ▬▬▬▬. Start from ⇨.

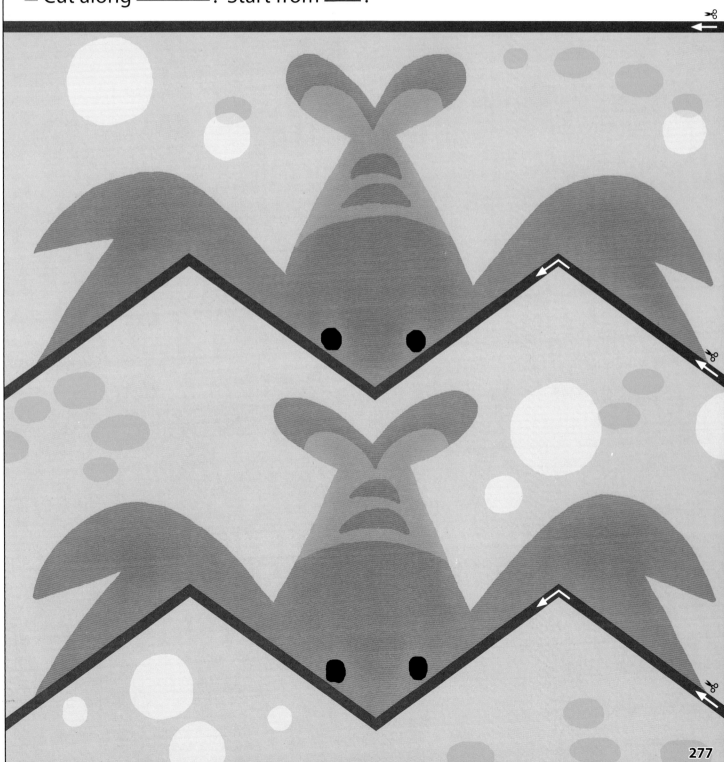

11 Gorilla

≪ example ≫

■ Cut along ▬▬▬. Start from ➡.

Beautiful Dress

To parents   In this exercise, your child will practice cutting wavy curves. It is okay for him or her to cut sharper angles at first. Remind your child to change direction a bit with each short stroke.

≪ example ≫

■ Cut along ▬▬▬▬. Start from ➡.

Whale Watching

To parents   Help your child open and close the scissors with short strokes in order to cut curves neatly. Through repeated practice, he or she will acquire stronger scissor control.

‹ example ›

■ Cut along ▬▬▬. Start from ⇒.

283

Snake

14

To parents   After your child has cut along the designated lines, hold the end up and let the cut portion fall down in a spiral. You can say something like, "Watch out for the snake!"

≪ example ≫

■ Cut along ▬▬▬▬ . Start from ➡ .

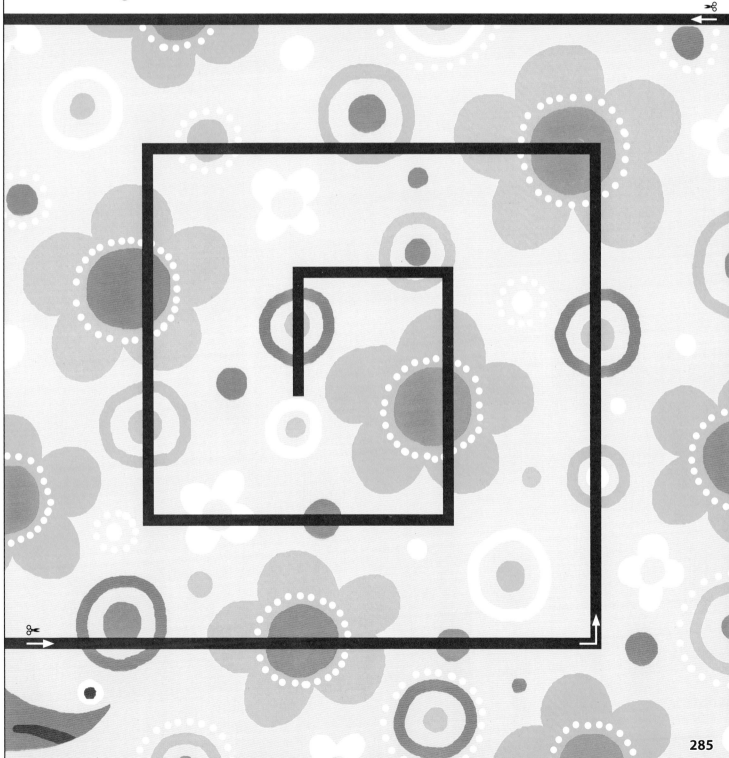

Let's Go Home

≪ example ≫

To parents It is important for your child to learn how to hold the paper with one hand while he or she cuts with the other hand. Help your child continue adjusting the paper in the right direction so that he or she is always holding the scissors straight.

■ Cut along ▬▬▬▬. Start from ■➡.

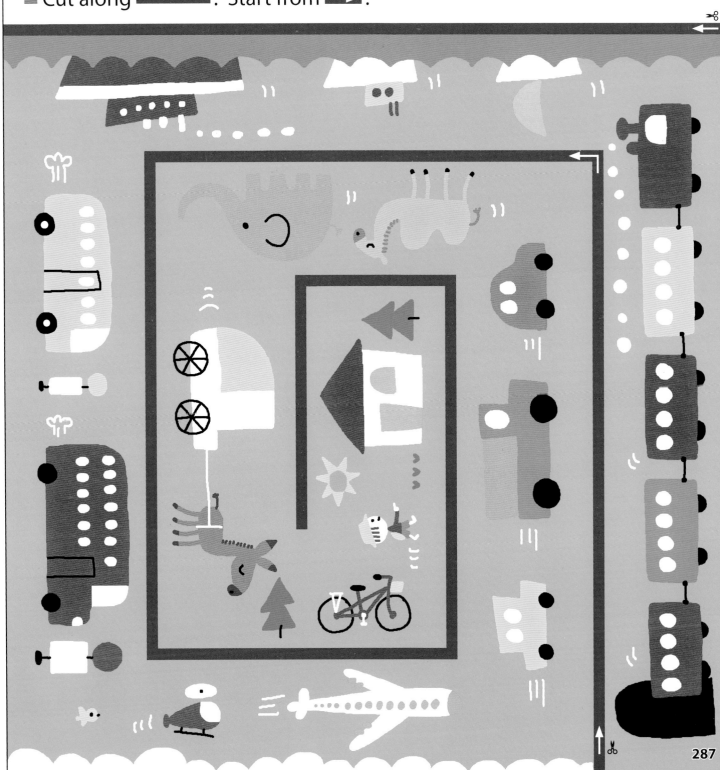

Catching a Fly

To parents In this exercise, your child must hold the paper and turn it while cutting. Make sure he or she is holding the scissors at the proper angle. After the exercise is done, your child can play with the lizard's swirling tongue.

⟨ example ⟩

■ Cut along ▬▬▬. Start from ➡.

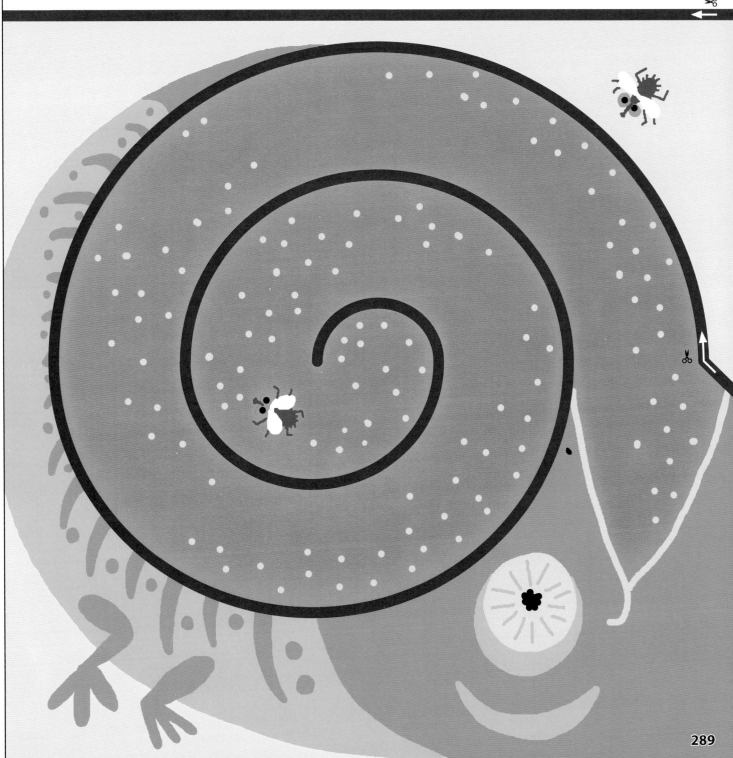

289

Swirling Noodles

< example >

To parents   This cutting line is longer than previous exercises. Your child will practice holding and turning the paper with one hand while cutting with the other hand. When your child is finished, offer lots of praise and encourage him or her to play with the swirling noodles.

■ Cut along ▬▬▬▬. Start from ⇒.

291

Breakfast Time

To parents From this page on, your child will cut out some parts. There is no starting line from the edge of the paper. If your child doesn't know where to begin cutting, tell him or her it is okay to start cutting from anywhere.

■ Cut along .

Lunch For Two

‹ example ›

To parents When your child has successfully finished, offer lots of praise. You can also use the pieces to pretend to have lunch with your child.

Cut along ▬▬▬ .

Elephant and Orangutan

≺ example ≻

To parents When your child cuts these round shapes, he or she will practice steadily turning the paper while cutting in order to make an evenly curved line. When your child has finished, you can play with the animals and ask, "What sounds do these animals make?"

■ Cut along ▬▬▬▬ .

Track Meet

To parents Don't be concerned if your child goes off the cutting line or cuts unevenly. When he or she is finished, offer lots of praise.

≪ example ≫

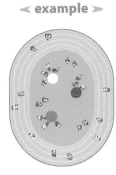

■ Cut along ▬▬▬▬ .

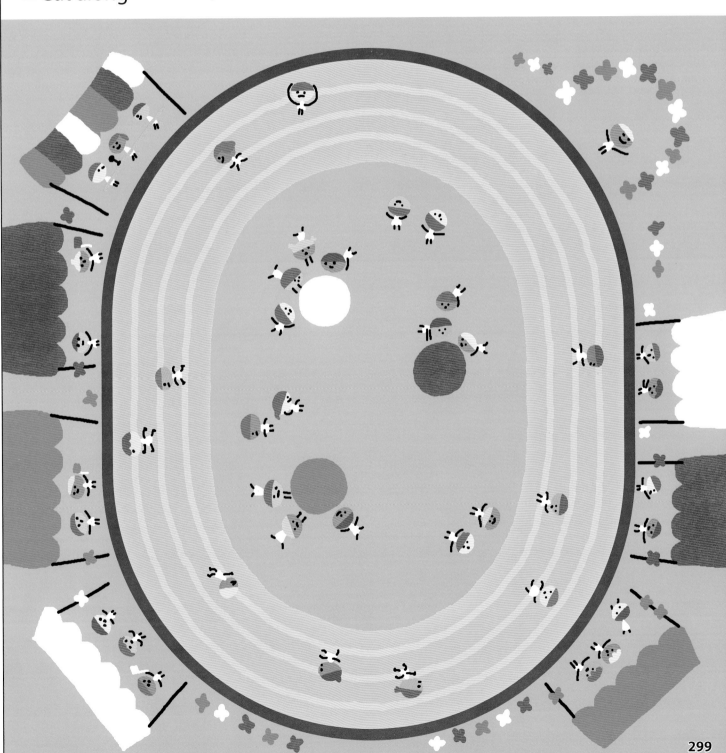

Thanksgiving

To parents From this page on, your child will cut out familiar objects. This illustration has an intricate shape. If your child does not cut the turkey perfectly, don't be concerned. When your child is finished, offer a lot of praise.

≪ example ≫

■ Cut along ▬▬▬ .

Halloween

To parents Please make sure your child is holding the scissors at the proper angle to the paper. Encourage your child to cut the pumpkin slowly and steadily.

■ Cut along ▬▬▬ .

24 Camping

≪ example ≫

To parents In this exercise, your child will cut out some parts. If your child doesn't know where to begin cutting, tell him or her it is okay to start from anywhere. When your child is finished, offer him or her a lot of praise and play with the tent's folding flap door.

■ Cut along ▬▬▬ and fold along —·—.

Christmas Tree

To parents   If your child is cutting into the picture, help him or her adjust the scissor's direction. Even if he or she cuts too far, you can always mend the paper with tape. When the Christmas tree is cut out, display it in your home.

■ Cut along ▬▬▬ .

Circus

‹ example ›

To parents From this page on, each exercise is two pages. Your child will cut out all the parts on the first page, and then he or she can display them in the scene on the second page.

■ Cut along ▬▬▬ and fold along ‒ ‒ ‒.
Then, stand the parts on the circus stage on the next page.

Circus

To parents On this page, your child can place the pieces wherever he or she likes. An example is offered but please allow your child to play freely.

<example>

■ Cut along ▬▬▬ and fold along ▬ ▪ ▬ ▪ ▬.

Playground

To parents In this exercise, your child will cut out the parts for the playground scene. These illustrations have very intricate shapes. If your child does not cut the shapes perfectly, don't be concerned. You can help him or her cut and fold. When your child is finished, offer a lot of praise.

≪ example ≫

■ Cut along ▬▬▬▬ and fold along ‒ ‒ ‒ .
  Then, stand the parts on the playground on the next page.

Playground

To parents On this page, your child will cut out the setting and place the pieces on the playground. There are many ways to place the pieces. Encourage your child to have fun by placing the parts in different arrangements.

‹ example ›

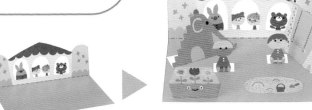

■ Cut along ▬▬▬ and fold along —·—.

In Town

To parents This is the last page in this section. When your child is finished, compare this page with his or her previous work. You will see a lot of progress in your child's ability to use scissors.

■ Cut along ▬▬▬ and fold along – – –.
Then, stand the parts on the roundabout on the next page.

In Town

◄ example ►

To parents Please encourage your child to place the parts wherever he or she likes. When the exercise is finished, remember to praise your child for his or her hard work.

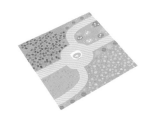

■ Cut along ▬▬▬▬ .

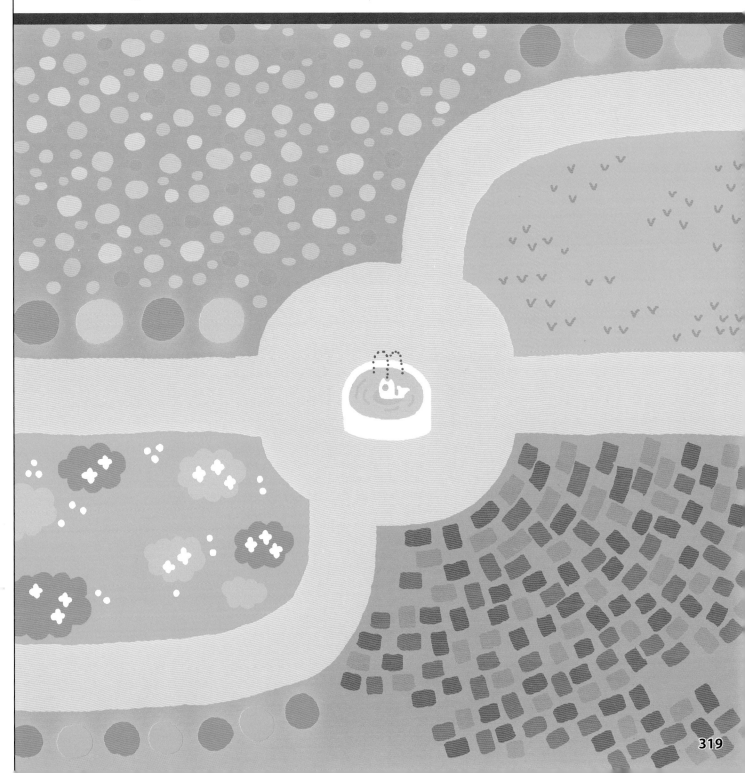

Are You Ready for Kindergarten?

Pasting Skills

To parents: Pasting Skills

In this section your child will complete activities designed to help him or her master pasting skills. This practice will help develop your child's fine motor control skills. This section allows your child to develop spatial reasoning and motor control skills, which are necessary for using other tools such as scissors.

First, your child will practice pasting simple shapes in any orientation on the page. Gradually, your child will paste multiple shapes in a particular orientation in order to fit a designated space. This incremental progress enables children to advance their motor control skills and spatial reasoning with confidence. Practicing pasting is fun and will enhance your child's awareness of shapes as well.

Parent Note: The pages in this section are designed to be removed from the book before your child completes them. Please cut the pages out of the workbook before you give them to your child to work on.

This skill will take plenty of practice to master. If your child struggles with any particular part of this section, please refer to the appropriate book from our other preschool products for more focused work.

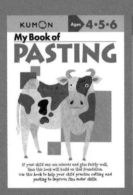
My Book of PASTING

Let's Sticker & Paste!

MORE Let's Sticker & Paste!

Let's Sticker & Paste! Amazing Animals

Let's Sticker & Paste! Food Fun

How to choose glue and how to paste

Please choose a child-safe product in an easy-to-use container. Your child can use a glue stick but it is best for children to use glue that can be applied by hand. Children enjoy the tactile experience of spreading glue with their fingers.

Line your table with scrap paper before your child starts. Have your child apply an appropriate amount of glue onto the tip of his or her finger and then spread it thinly on the paper object to be pasted. Please put the glue on the side with the glue symbol.

When your child is first attempting to paste, encourage him or her to place the edges of the paper object down first and then slowly press the rest of the object into place. Your child will gradually learn how to align the object correctly.
In the beginning, do not worry too much if your child cannot paste accurately. Observe your child's progress, and encourage him or her to advance one step at a time.

My Desk

To parents First, your child will practice pasting with glue. Please cut out the part below for your child. If your child wants to cut it independently, that is okay too. Please assist your child and keep an eye on him or her to avoid any injuries.

■ Paste the cut out part onto the desk.

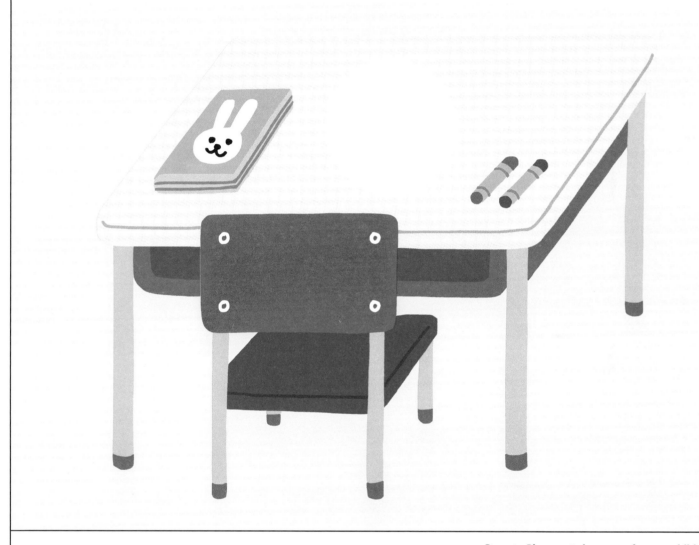

Parents: Please cut along —— for your child.

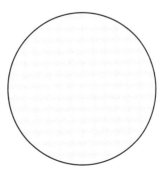

Parents: Please cut this part out for your child.

323

Up and Down the Slide

< example >

To parents   In this exercise, your child will paste the square. Don't be concerned if the cut out piece isn't perfectly placed onto the picture. The most important thing is that your child enjoys pasting with glue.

■ Paste the cut out part onto the slide.

Parents: Please cut along —— for your child.

Parents: Please cut this part out for your child.

325

Big Tree

To parents Your child will paste the oval. Encourage your child to pay attention to the orientation of the shape.

≪ example ≫

■ Paste the cut out part onto the tree.

Parents: Please cut along —— for your child.

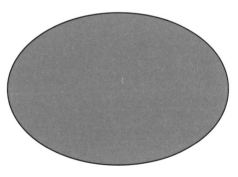

Parents: Please cut this part out for your child.

Seesaw

To parents On this page your child will paste the rectangle. Encourage your child to pay attention to the orientation of the shape.

■ Paste the cut out part onto the seesaw.

Parents: Please cut along —— for your child.

Parents: Please cut this part out for your child.

329

Turtles In a Pond

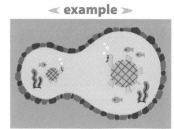

‹ example ›

■ Paste the cut out part onto the pond.

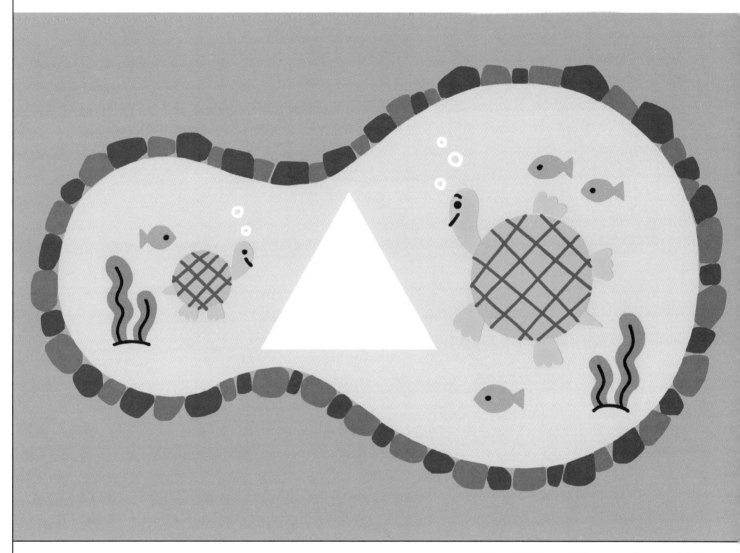

Parents: Please cut along ——— for your child.

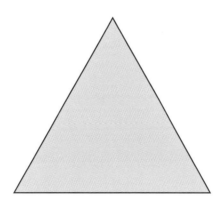

Parents: Please cut this part out for your child.

Kindergarten

< example >

To parents Your child should be careful to correctly align the piece. If he or she doesn't know the proper orientation, please offer to help.

■ Paste the cut out part onto the roof.

Parents: Please cut along —— for your child.

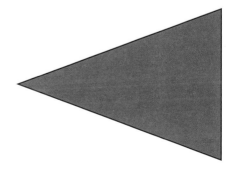

Parents: Please cut this part out for your child.

My Bag

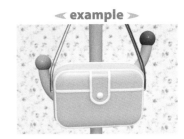

To parents From this page on, your child will practice pasting to complete the design in the picture.
If the piece isn't placed onto the picture neatly, don't be concerned.

■ Paste the cut out part onto the bag.

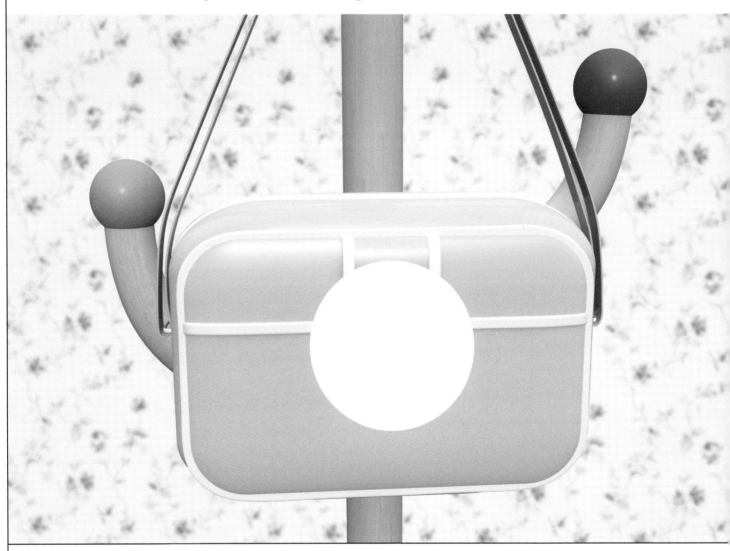

Parents: Please cut along ——— for your child.

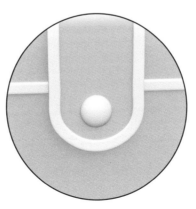

Parents: Please cut this part out for your child.

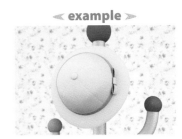
8 **My Hat**

To parents The most important thing is that your child enjoys pasting. When he or she is finished, talk about the hats your child likes to wear.

■ Paste the cut out part onto the hat.

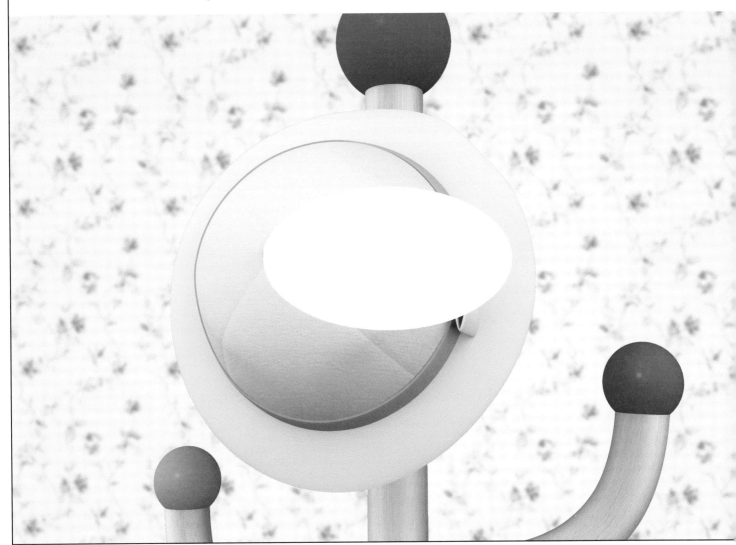

Parents: Please cut along —— for your child.

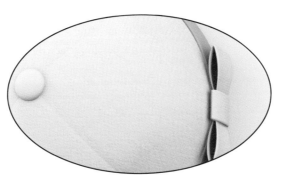

Parents: Please cut this part out for your child.

Bear's Mug

To parents On this page your child must paste the piece with the bear's face in the correct orientation. It helps to discuss the proper placement with your child before he or she pastes the part.

■ Paste the cut out part onto the mug.

Parents: Please cut along ⎯⎯ for your child.

Parents: Please cut this part out for your child.

Frog's Umbrella

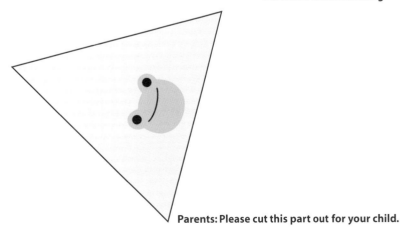

To parents This exercise encourages your child to practice pasting parts with the correct orientation. Please help your child place the frog's face in the appropriate position.

■ Paste the cut out part onto the umbrella.

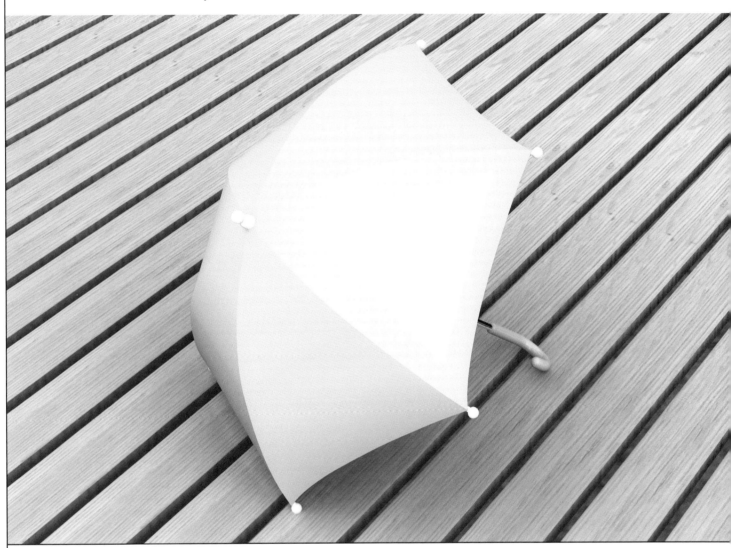

Parents: Please cut along ——— for your child.

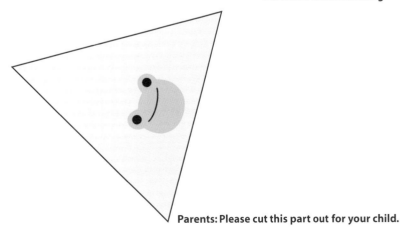

Parents: Please cut this part out for your child.

Rabbit's Towel

< example >

To parents This towel has an intricate pattern. If the pattern on the towel doesn't perfectly match the pasted part, don't be concerned. When your child is finished, offer a lot of praise.

■ Paste the cut out part onto the towel.

Parents: Please cut along —— for your child.

Parents: Please cut this part out for your child.

Frog's Rain Boots

To parents   Your child will paste the piece to complete the rain boots. It is difficult to perfectly match the illustration. If it isn't correctly placed onto the picture, don't be concerned.

■ Paste the cut out part onto the rain boots.

Parents: Please cut along ——— for your child.

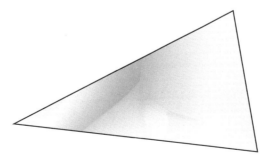

Parents: Please cut this part out for your child.

Playing Ball

To parents From this page on, your child will practice pasting pieces onto the page wherever he or she likes. An example is offered but please allow your child to paste freely.

≪ example ≫

■ Paste the ball as you like.

Parents: Please cut along —— for your child.

Parents: Please cut this part out for your child.

Drawing a Picture

≺ example ≻

To parents In this exercise your child will paste the crayons onto the desk. If your child doesn't know where to place the piece, offer to help.

■ Paste the crayons on the desk as you like.

Parents: Please cut along —— for your child.

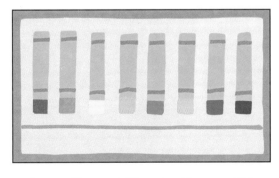

Parents: Please cut this part out for your child.

15 Put the Shoes Away

To parents Your child will paste the shoes onto the cubby. There are more empty cubbyholes than the amount of pieces. Encourage your child to paste the shoes on whichever empty cubbyholes that he or she likes.

■ Paste the shoes onto the cubby as you like.

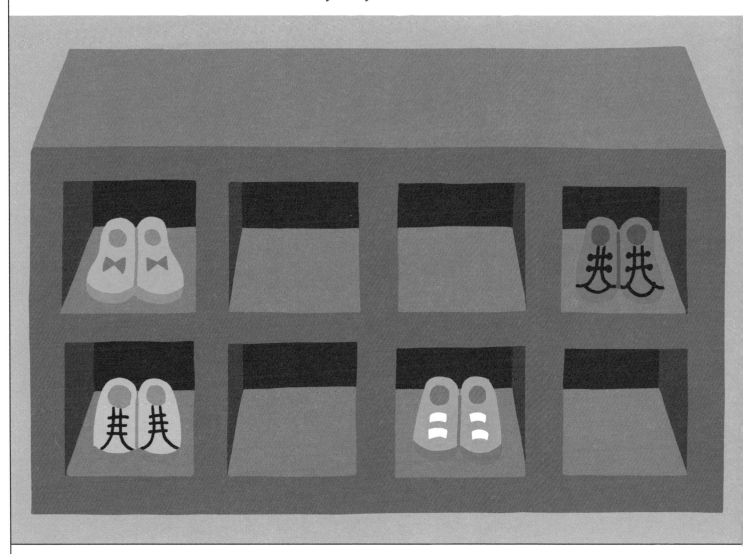

Parents: Please cut along —— for your child.

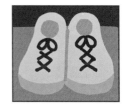

Parents: Please cut these parts out for your child.

16 Birthday Party

≪ example ≫

To parents If your child doesn't know where to place the piece, ask, "Who is not wearing a hat?"
Please remember to praise your child for his or her hard work.

■ Paste the hats as you like.

Parents: Please cut along —— for your child.

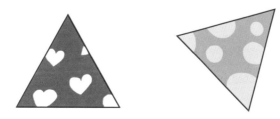

Parents: Please cut these parts out for your child.

Let's Get Dressed

≪ example ≫

To parents   Your child will paste the clothes, hat and shoes. When he or she is finished, offer a lot of praise and then say, "Can you put on your clothes by yourself?"

■ Paste the clothes onto the boy.

Parents: Please cut along —— for your child.

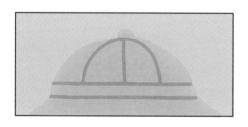

Parents: Please cut these parts out for your child.

Art Supplies

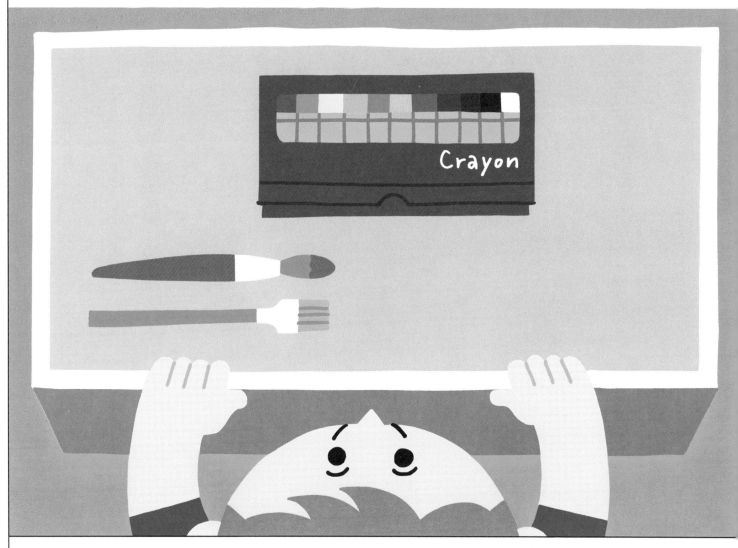

To parents   Your child will paste the art supplies as though they are putting the items away in the box. When he or she is finished, offer a lot of praise, such as, "You put the supplies away very well."

■ Paste the craft supplies into the box as you like.

Parents: Please cut along —— for your child.

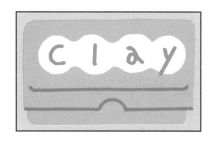

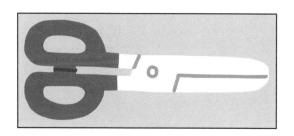

Parents: Please cut these parts out for your child.

19 Put the Toys Away

< example >

To parents Your child will paste the toys and books onto the cubby. Please encourage your child to paste them wherever he or she likes. When your child is finished, offer a lot of praise, such as, "You put the toys away very well."

■ Paste the cut out parts onto the cubby as you like.

Parents: Please cut along —— for your child.

Parents: Please cut these parts out for your child.

What Time Is It Now?

≺ example ≻

To parents Your child will paste the numbers onto the clock. If he or she doesn't know the correct place to paste each number, offer to help. When the clock is finished, read the numbers in order to your child and talk about the time.

■ Paste the numbers onto the clock.

Parents: Please cut along —— for your child.

Parents: Please cut these parts out for your child.

Lunchbox

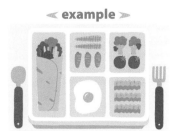

To parents Your child will paste the food onto the lunchbox. These pieces are equal in size, so your child can paste them wherever he or she likes. When the exercise is finished, ask your child about his or her favorite lunch food.

■ Paste the dishes onto the lunchbox as you like.

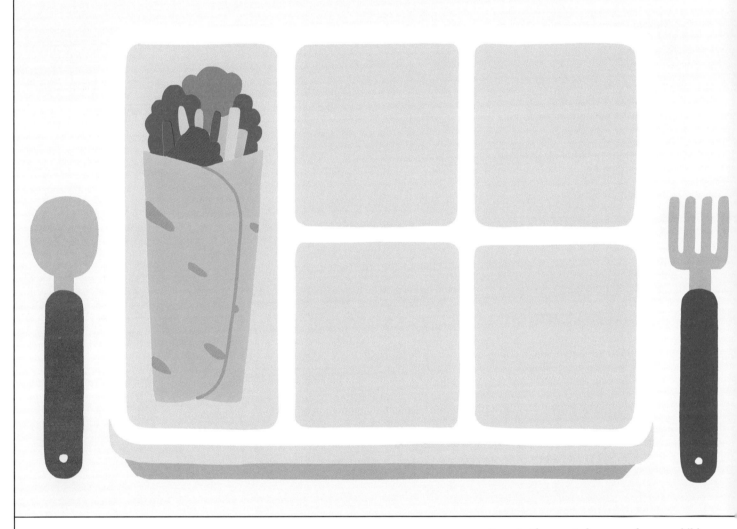

Parents: Please cut along —— for your child.

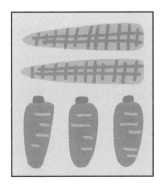
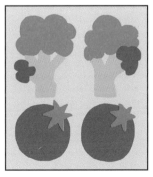

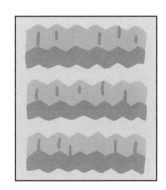

Parents: Please cut these parts out for your child.

363

Mother's Day

≪ example ≫

To parents From this page on, your child will paste the parts as though he or she is completing a puzzle. If your child doesn't know the correct way to paste each part, offer to help. When he or she is finished, offer a lot of praise, such as "Wow! You did a great job!"

■ Paste the cut out parts to complete the picture.

Parents: Please cut along —— for your child.

Parents: Please cut this part out for your child.

Parents: Please cut along —— for your child.

365

4TH of July

To parents   In this exercise, your child will paste the parts to complete the scene. Encourage your child to try different placements before using glue. When he or she is finished, offer a lot of praise and ask, "Do you like fireworks?"

■ Paste the cut out parts to complete the picture.

Parents: Please cut along —— for your child.

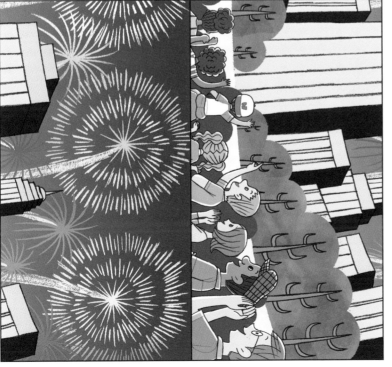

Parents: Please cut these parts out for your child.

Earth Day

< example >
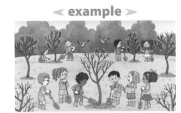

To parents Your child will paste the parts to complete the scene. Encourage your child to pay attention to the orientation and alignment. When he or she is finished, you can talk about how you celebrate Earth Day.

■ Paste the cut out parts to complete the picture.

Parents: Please cut along ——— for your child.

Parents: Please cut these parts out for your child.

Halloween

To parents Your child should be careful to correctly place and align the parts. If he or she doesn't know the proper position and orientation, please offer to help.

■ Paste the cut out parts to complete the picture.

Parents: Please cut these parts out for your child.   Parents: Please cut along —— for your child.

New Year's Eve

To parents It is difficult to perfectly align the details of the illustration. So, don't be concerned if the parts are not aligned correctly. Offer your child a lot of praise and say, "New Year's Eve looks like fun!"

■ Paste the cut out parts to complete the picture.

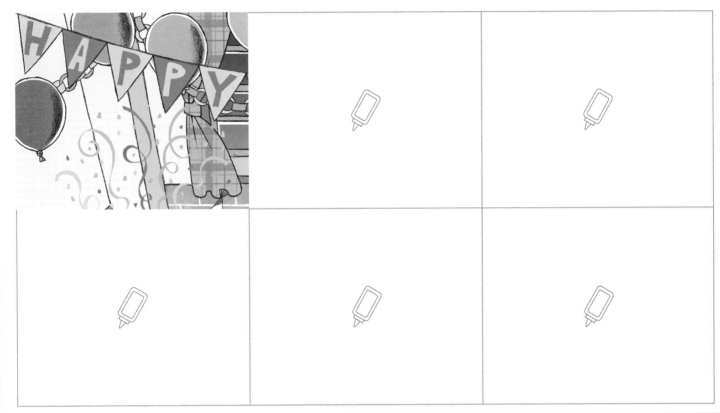

Parents: Please cut along —— for your child.

Parents: Please cut these parts out for your child.

27 Thanksgiving

<< example >>

To parents In this exercise, your child will paste all the parts to create the illustration. If your child doesn't know where to place the pieces, offer to help.

■ Paste the cut out parts to complete the picture.

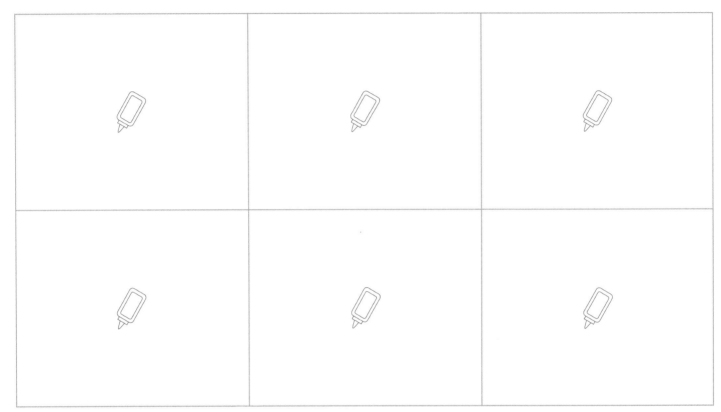

Parents: Please cut these parts out for your child.

Parents: Please cut along —— for your child.

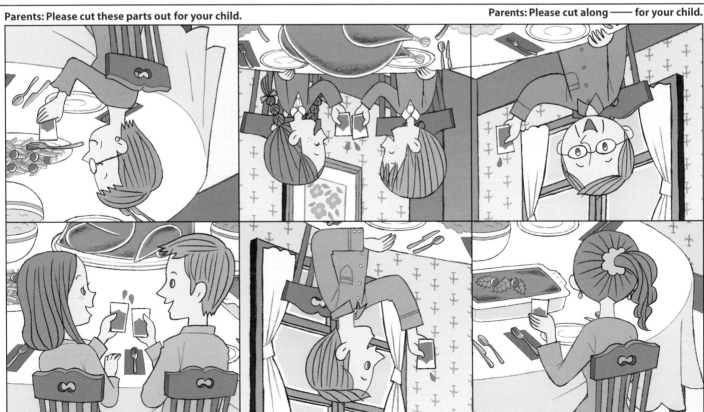

28 Valentine's Day

< example >

To parents This illustration has a lot of intricate details. If the parts are not perfectly aligned, don't be concerned. When your child is finished, offer a lot of praise.

■ Paste the cut out parts to complete the picture.

Parents: Please cut these parts out for your child.

Parents: Please cut along —— for your child.

29 Home Sweet Home

≪ example ≫

■ Paste the cut out parts to complete the picture.

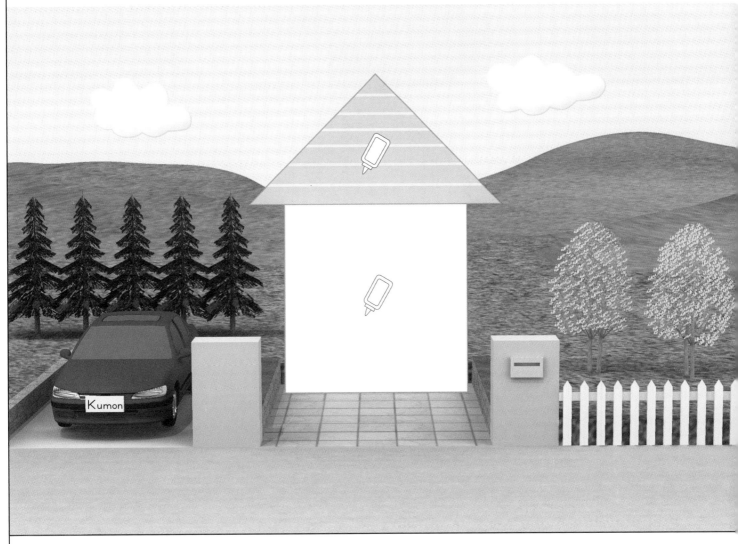

Parents: Please cut along —— for your child.

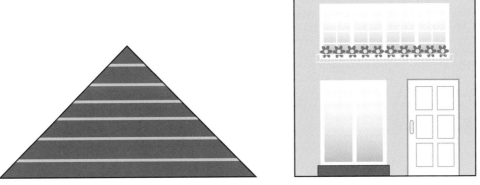

Parents: Please cut these parts out for your child.

Super Express Train

< example >

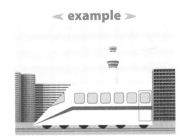

To parents This is the last page in the workbook, remember to praise your child for his or her hard work. Your child will make a train with three pieces. If he or she is unsure of where to place each piece, encourage your child to look at the example.

■ Paste the cut out parts to complete the picture.

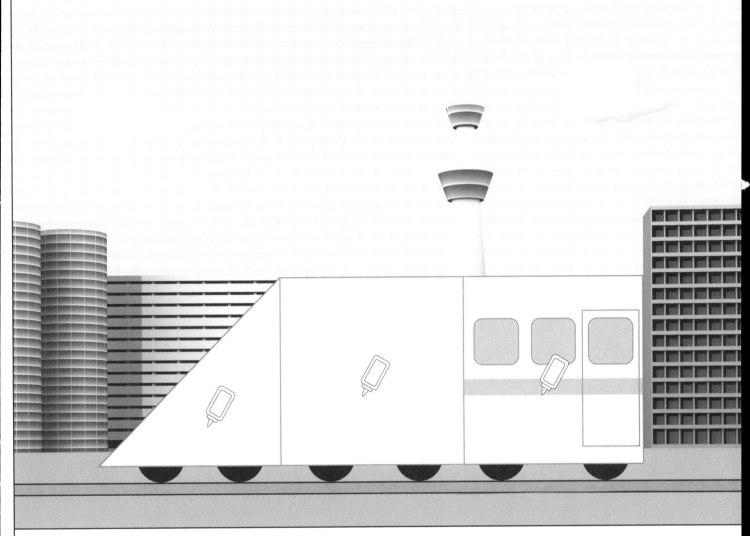

Parents: Please cut along ——— for your child.

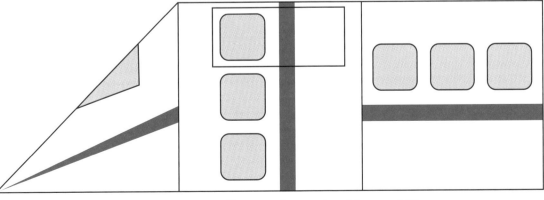

Parents: Please cut these parts out for your child.

KUM⊙N

Certificate of

Achievement

5A

is hereby congratulated on completing

Are You Ready for Kindergarten?

Presented on

, 20

Parent or Guardian